This book belongs to

_____

_____

GUIDE *to* ONGOING FORMATION *for* PRIESTS

UNITED STATES
CONFERENCE OF
CATHOLIC BISHOPS

GUIDE *to* ONGOING FORMATION *for* PRIESTS

A letter from the bishops
of the United States to priests

ASCENSION
West Chester, Pennsylvania

The document *Guide to Ongoing Formation for Priests* was developed by the Committee on Clergy, Consecrated Life and Vocations of the United States Conference of Catholic Bishops (USCCB). It was approved by the full body of bishops at its June 2023 Plenary Assembly and has been authorized for publication by the undersigned.

Fr. Michael Fuller, S.Th.D.
General Secretary, USCCB

ISBN: 978-1-954882-63-8

This edition © 2023 Ascension Publishing Group, LLC.
Published under license granted by the United States Conference of Catholic Bishops.

Ascension
PO Box 1990
West Chester, PA 19380
1-800-376-0520
ascensionpress.com

Printed in the United States of America
24 25 26 27 28 6 5 4 3 2

— CONTENTS —

FOREWORD 1

INTRODUCTION (NOS. 1-13) 3

CHAPTER 1: PRIESTLY LIFE (NOS. 14-59) 8
Description of a Holy, Healthy Priesthood *(nos. 18-43)* 9
  Christian Identity (nos. 18-24) 9
  Masculine Identity (nos. 25-30) 12
  Priestly Identity (nos. 31-39) 14
  Dedication to a Life of Learning and Growing (nos. 40-43) 19
Challenges to Living the Priesthood Today *(nos. 44-59)* 21
  Within the Priesthood (nos. 47-51) 22
  Within the Church (nos. 52-54) 24
  From the Wider Culture (nos. 55-59) 25

CHAPTER 2: ONGOING FORMATION (NOS. 60-103) 28
Formation Is a Lifelong Process *(nos. 64-69)* 29
  Growth Is a Sign of Life (nos. 64-66) 29
  Post-Seminary Formation (nos. 67-69) 30
Means for Ongoing Formation (nos. 70-86) 32
  Personal Means (nos. 71-74) 33
  Fraternal Means (nos. 75-81) 34
  Episcopal Means (nos. 82-84) 38
  Aids to Personal, Fraternal, and Episcopal Means (nos. 85-86) 39
Ongoing Formation at Different Stages of Life *(nos. 87-103)* 40
  Early Priesthood (nos. 89-92) 41
  Transitions (nos. 93-97) 43
  Middle Years of Priesthood (nos. 98-99) 44
  Senior and "Retired" Clergy (nos. 100-103) 45

Chapter 3: Human Formation (nos. 104-144) 47

Markers of the Human Dimension *(nos. 107-132)* 48

Human Maturity (nos. 107-110) 48

Unity of Life (nos. 111-113) 49

Capacity for Fatherhood (no. 114) 51

Healthy Chastity (nos. 115-120) 53

Capacity for Friendship (nos. 121-127) 56

Temperance (nos. 128-132) 58

Means of Human Formation *(nos. 133-144)* 61

Personal Means (nos. 133-137) 61

Fraternal Means (nos. 138-142) 62

Episcopal Means (nos. 143-144) 64

Chapter 4: Spiritual Formation (nos. 145-179) 66

Markers of the Spiritual Dimension *(nos. 150-160)* 67

Awareness of God's Love (nos. 150-151) 67

Union with the Sacrifice of Christ (no. 152) 68

Pursuit of Holiness (nos. 153-156) 69

Fidelity to the Church (nos. 157-160) 71

Means of Spiritual Formation *(nos. 161-179)* 73

Personal Means (nos. 161-172) 73

Fraternal Means (nos. 173-175) 79

Episcopal Means (nos. 176-179) 80

Chapter 5: Intellectual Formation (nos. 180-205) 82

Markers of the Intellectual Dimension *(nos. 190-195)* 85

Catechetical and Theological Competence (nos. 190-191) 85

Engagement with the World (nos. 192-193) 86

Thirst for Intellectual Growth (nos. 194-195) 87

Means of Intellectual Formation *(nos. 196-205)* 88

Personal Means (nos. 196-200) 88

Fraternal Means (nos. 201-202) 90

Episcopal Means (nos. 203-205) 91

CHAPTER 6: PASTORAL FORMATION (NOS. 206-238) 93

Markers of the Pastoral Dimension *(nos. 210-223)* 95

Freedom for Ministry (nos. 210-213) 95

Spiritual Sonship (no. 214) 96

Primacy Given to Salvation of Souls (nos. 215-219) 97

A Heart Open to All (nos. 220-223) 101

Means of Pastoral Formation *(nos. 224-238)* 103

Personal Means (nos. 224-229) 103

Fraternal Means (nos. 230-232) 107

Episcopal Means (nos. 233-238) 108

Priestly Ministry *(nos. 234-236)* 108

Parish Apostolates *(no. 237)* 110

Management *(no. 238)* 110

APPENDIX A. PROGRAM *for* NEWLY ORDAINED PRIESTS

(NOS. 239-259) 112

Preliminary Observations *(nos. 240-242)* 112

Part 1: Key Leadership in the Ongoing Formation of the

Recently Ordained Priest *(nos. 243-249)* 114

The Diocesan Bishop (no. 244) 114

The Pastor (nos. 245-246) 114

The Spiritual Director (no. 247) 116

The Mentor (no. 248) 116

The Director (no. 249) 117

Part 2: Key Programming in the Ongoing Formation of the

Recently Ordained Priest *(nos. 250-258)* 118

Retreats and Times of Recollection (no. 251) 118

Attention to Physical Health and Emotional Well-Being
(nos. 252-253) 119

Pastoral and Human Formation (nos. 254-255) 119

Special Consideration (no. 256) 121

Orientation for Pastors and Mentors (nos. 257-258) 121

Final Note *(no. 259)* 122

APPENDIX B. A TOOL *to* EVALUATE WHEN *a* PRIEST
REQUIRES ASSISTANCE (NOS. 260-280) 123

A Priest's Health Inventory *(nos. 261-278)* 123

Physical Health Problems (nos. 262-265) 123

Emotional Health Problems (nos. 266-268) 124

Social Support Problems (nos. 269-271) 125

Ministerial Environment Problems (nos. 272-274) 126

Spiritual Health Problems (nos. 275-278) 126

A Priest's Health Analysis *(nos. 279-280)* 127

APPENDIX C. CULTURAL CONSIDERATIONS *in*
ONGOING FORMATION (NOS. 281-301) 128

Context *(nos. 281-283)* 128

The Power of Culture *(nos. 284-286)* 129

The Power of Faith *(no. 287)* 130

Cultural Orientation *(no. 288)* 131

Culture and Ongoing Formation *(no. 289)* 131

Boundary Education *(no. 290)* 132

Intercultural Competency *(nos. 291-293)* 132

Language Acquisition and Accent Modification *(nos. 294-295)* 134

Cultural Sensitivity Observations *(nos. 296-300)* 135

Culture and Planning *(no. 301)* 137

APPENDIX D. BOUNDARY EDUCATION (NOS. 302-313) 138

Health and Boundaries *(no. 304)* 138

Protection of Youth *(no. 305)* 139

Protection of Vulnerable Adults *(no. 306)* 139

Reporting *(no. 307)* 140

Ministry Boundaries *(no. 308)* 140

Workplace Boundaries *(no. 309)* 141

Boundaries with Adults Outside Ministry
and the Workplace *(no. 310)* 141

Boundaries in the Physical Environment *(no. 311)* 141

Professional and Financial Boundaries *(no. 312)* 142

Boundaries in Communications *(no. 313)* 143

Note: The numbers appearing at the top corner of each page
refer to paragraph numbers of the text.

FOREWORD

The development of this *Guide to Ongoing Formation for Priests* began in October 2020. Under the leadership of Bishop James Checchio, Chair, the Committee on Clergy, Consecrated Life and Vocations (CCLV) formed a working group to draft the document. Members of the working group included Bishop Daniel Mueggenborg, Chair; Bishop Richard Henning; Very Rev. John McCrone; Rev. Jeff Eirvin; Rev. Carter Griffin; Rev. David Songy, O.F.M. Cap; Deacon Steven DeMartino; and Sr. Mary Joanna Ruhland, RSM. Rev. Jorge Torres, Rev. Luke Ballman, and Rev. Daniel Hanley of the CCLV Secretariat supported the working group. Feedback from the body of bishops during the regional meetings of the June 2021 Plenary Assembly and CCLV's collaborating committees was incorporated into the draft completed in 2021.

The members of the CCLV Committee who brought this document to completion are Bishop Earl Boyea, Chair; Archbishop Charles Thompson; Bishop Juan Miguel Betancourt; Bishop François Beyrouti, Bishop Ronald Hicks, Bishop David Toups, Bishop Austin Vetter, and Bishop William Wack.

Complementary to the *Program of Priestly Formation*, sixth edition, this document aligns with the structure and paradigm of ongoing formation reflected in the *Ratio Fundamentalis Institutiones Sacerdotalis* (December 2016) and the *Directory for the Ministry and Life of Priests* (June 2013) by emphasizing personal, fraternal, and episcopal means of ongoing formation. It is a letter from the bishops of the United States to their priests. Its tone is pastoral, not programmatic, and its purpose is to suggest concrete means for priests, as the primary protagonists of their own formation, to continue their personal and priestly formation following their ordination to the priesthood. This *Guide* is meant to encourage priests to reflect on their life and ministry and formulate an individualized plan of formation in light of the current realities in the life of priests, society, and the Church. We encourage using this text in the context of dialogue with laity, brother priests and their bishops.

On behalf of the United States Conference of Catholic Bishops and the Committee on Clergy, Consecrated Life and Vocations, I extend my deepest gratitude to all those individuals who contributed to this project over the last three years. May Mary, the Mother of God and Queen of Apostles, and St. John Vianney, patron saint of priests, intercede for all priests so that they may continue to conform their lives to the image of Christ, the Good Shepherd in service to the Gospel.

✠ Bishop Earl Boyea
Chairman, Committee on Clergy,
Consecrated Life and Vocations

INTRODUCTION

1 One of the warmest friendships in all Scripture is that between St. Paul and St. Timothy. Paul had known Timothy from his youth and was like a father to him. "I yearn to see you again," Paul wrote to him, "recalling your tears, so that I may be filled with joy, as I recall your sincere faith that first lived in your grandmother Lois and in your mother Eunice and that I am confident lives also in you" (2 Tm 1:4-5).

2 St. Timothy spent years in the company of St. Paul during his missionary voyages, being formed in the faith and in apostolic ministry. Eventually Paul left Timothy in Ephesus as a newly ordained bishop, but he continued to reach out to his spiritual son with paternal love and concern. Paul advised, inspired, and exhorted his "dear child" to live out the sacred office he received at his hands: "For this reason, I remind you to stir into flame the gift of God that you have through the imposition of my hands. For God did not give us a spirit of cowardice but rather of power and love and self-control. So do not be ashamed of your testimony to our Lord, nor of me, a prisoner for his sake; but bear your share of hardship for the gospel with the strength that comes from God" (2 Tm 1:6-8).

3 With Paul's departure, Timothy was working on his own in the vineyard of the Lord. His initial period of formation was complete, but his continued growth was no less urgent. As he cared for souls and preached the Gospel, Timothy continued to mature as a man, deepen his interior life, conform himself to God's will, expand his understanding of the faith, learn from his pastoral experience, and hone his capacity to preach and care for souls.

4   Countless priests through the ages have had experiences like Timothy's. Once their initial formation is complete, priests are sent into the vineyard to care for souls and preach the Gospel. Priests, often at a young age, are entrusted with weighty pastoral responsibilities, but they lack the structures of support that were present in their seminary community. As Paul foresaw in the life of Timothy, priests still find it necessary to "stir into flame the gift of God" that they received through the imposition of the bishop's hands.

5   Priestly renewal is a gift freely bestowed by God, and the priest bears the principal and primary responsibility for rekindling the grace of ordination as it belonged to Timothy.[1] Without the established means of formation that surrounded him in the seminary, the priest is now called to live in a way that allows the Lord to sustain his priesthood and help him grow in holiness and zeal. He needs to be proactive and intentional about his ongoing formation and must take concrete measures to live it out, because ongoing formation will not happen on its own. The consequences of failing to desire and engage in ongoing formation have been all too clear in recent decades.

6   The purpose of this document is to allow the Lord to continue to form priests in their personal and priestly formation. As bishops of the United States, we offer this document to our priests, our sons, who share the one priesthood of Jesus with us. We intend this *Guide* to help each priest to take stock of his life and ministry and to discern and formulate an individualized plan of formation.[2]

---

1   St. John Paul II, *Pastores Dabo Vobis (I Will Give You Shepherds)*, March 25, 1992, no. 23. Subsequently cited as PDV.

2   The 2001 *Basic Plan for the Ongoing Formation of Priests* was designed for bishops and their collaborators responsible for ongoing formation. This *Guide* is intended as a practical tool for the priests themselves, in the light of current realities in society and the Church. These include a prevailing secular ethos, moral relativism, fewer priests, a large Catholic population, loss of credibility for the Church, and an overall lack of respect for religion due to the scandalous and criminal behavior of some clergy who have abused minors and engaged in sexual misconduct with adults (including seminarians), among other realities.

7   It is hoped that this document will be useful for diocesan priests, those members of religious institutes and societies of apostolic life, and priests who have professed other forms of consecrated life. As St. Pope John Paul II states in *Vita Consecrata*,

> Due to human limitations, the consecrated person can never claim to have completely brought to life the "new creature" who, in every circumstance of life, reflects the very mind of Christ. . . . None are exempt from the obligation to grow humanly and as Religious; by the same token, no one can be over-confident and live in self-sufficient isolation. At no stage of life can people feel so secure and committed that they do not need to give careful attention to ensuring perseverance in faithfulness; just as there is no age at which a person has completely achieved maturity.[3]

8   This practical *Guide* is not meant to be an exposition on the meaning and identity of the priesthood or a theological treatment of priestly spirituality. Those themes are explored more explicitly in the *2013 Directory for the Ministry and Life of Priests* (DMLP) from the Congregation for the Clergy.[4] In fact, the present document can be considered a companion to the DMLP, drawing from it liberally and presupposing its theological and pastoral insights. The purpose of this document is to help priests apply its wisdom in their lives.[5] It is a pastoral document and is not particular law for the United States. However, it is to be interpreted in accord with church teaching

---

3   St. John Paul II, *Vita Consecrata (On the Consecrated Life and Its Mission in the Church and in the World)* March 25, 1996, no. 69.

4   Congregation for the Clergy, *Directory for the Ministry and the Life of Priests* (DMLP), new ed. (Vatican City: Libreria Editrice Vaticana, 2013), no. 87. Subsequently cited as DMLP.

5   Priests who are consecrated may benefit also from Pope St. John Paul II's apostolic exhortation *Vita Consecrata* and from the Congregation for Institutes of Consecrated Life and Societies of Apostolic Life.

regarding faith and morals, the *Code of Canon Law*, and other church laws, both universal and particular.[6]

9   This document follows the structure established by Pope St. John Paul II in *Pastores Dabo Vobis* and taken up by the *Ratio Fundamentalis Institutionis Sacerdotalis* and the *Program of Priestly Formation* of the United States Conference of Catholic Bishops (USCCB).[7] Just as seminary formation is arranged under the four dimensions of formation—human, spiritual, intellectual, and pastoral—so too are these dimensions a helpful framework for the ongoing formation of priests. Chapter one sketches the goal of ongoing formation: a thriving and fruitful priesthood. Chapter two shows ongoing formation to be a lifelong process and identifies the ordinary means to pursue it. The bulk of this document, however, explores the four dimensions of formation in turn. Chapters three through six single out markers for growth in their respective dimensions as well as personal, fraternal, and episcopal means to grow in those dimensions.[8]

10   This document can be used in a variety of ways. Priests will find it helpful to review the document regularly, so that new avenues of growth are never lacking. Specific resolutions to improve are essential to any plan of ongoing formation. Priests are urged to discuss these resolutions in spiritual direction and with priest friends and mentors.

---

6   See *Code of Canon Law (Codex Iuris Canonici [CIC])*. cc. 276, §2, 4°, and 279 §2. Subsequently cited as CIC.

7   Congregation for the Clergy, *Ratio Fundamentalis Institutionis Sacerdotalis (The Gift of the Priestly Vocation)* (Vatican City: L'Osservatore Romano, 2016), no. 81. Subsequently cited as *Ratio Fundamentalis*. United States Conference of Catholic Bishops (USCCB), *Program for Priestly Formation* in the United States, 6th ed., Washington, DC: USCCB, 2022. Hereafter cited as PPF.

8   Personal, fraternal, and episcopal means are envisioned by the *Ratio Fundamentalis* and the PPF. "After all, it is the priest himself who is principally and primarily responsible for his own ongoing formation. . . . Priestly fraternity is the first setting in which ongoing formation takes place." *Ratio Fundamentalis*, no. 82. "This journey of discipleship and growth in Christian faith and service continues after ordination with ongoing formation, in which the ordained priest seeks an ever-deepening conformity to Christ under the guidance of the diocesan bishop or competent authority of the institute of consecrated life or society of apostolic life." PPF, no. 33.

11 The document can also be profitably used in fraternal discussions. The insights of fellow priests, each striving to grow, can be mutually illuminating and encouraging. Such discussions are best held in the context of prayerful fraternity.

12 Finally, although the main body of this document can be useful to those formally entrusted with the care of priests, the appendices are specifically aimed at those involved in ongoing clergy formation at the diocesan level.[9] Each of the four appendices focuses on a topic deemed to merit a more detailed treatment: respectively, programs for recently ordained priests, tools for evaluating when clergy require assistance, cultural considerations in ongoing formation, and boundary education.

13 As priests of the United States, you give of yourselves generously and faithfully in serving the people in your care. Often enough, you do so at the expense of your own needs and personal growth. Our heartfelt prayer as your bishops is that these pages will help right that imbalance and provide tangible help in the lives of you, our priests, who wish to "stir into flame the gift of God" that you received at ordination. May that rekindled flame burn brightly and warm innumerable souls on their journey to their heavenly home.

---

9   Although this *Guide* is directed specifically to priests of the Latin Church, it may assist all Churches *sui iuris* in the United States when adapted to reflect the traditions, pastoral life, and requirements of the *Code of Canons of the Eastern Churches.*

CHAPTER ONE
PRIESTLY LIFE

14　Jesus once compared the Kingdom of God to a man sowing seed: "It is as if a man were to scatter seed on the land and would sleep and rise night and day and the seed would sprout and grow, he knows not how" (Mk 4:26-27). Seeds have a mysterious principle of life that causes them to grow and bear fruit as a matter of course, as long as they are planted in good soil that is rich in nutrients and are nourished with water and sunlight.

15　What Jesus attributed to the Kingdom of God is also present in the priesthood. The priestly vocation has an inner principle of life that—planted in good soil and nourished by grace—"sprouts and grows" in a fruitful way. Ongoing formation means making space for this inner principle of life to flourish.[10] It is more than personal or professional development. It means providing the right environment for growth, tilling the soil, ensuring good nourishment, uprooting weeds, and clearing away rocks.[11] The seed of the priestly vocation, which is the gift of God, will take care of the rest.

16　To continue the analogy, farmers plant seeds with a goal in mind. They want seeds to flourish and become mature crops that bear a rich harvest. Growth, in other words, is ordered to an end; the desired end is how farmers gauge the quality of growth. This document begins its treatment of ongoing formation by examining the end to which priestly growth is directed. We describe the kind of priesthood that is fruitful, rich in meaning, integrated, and joyful. The features of such a

---

10　"Ongoing formation is intended to ensure fidelity to priestly ministry in a continuing journey of conversion, in order to rekindle the gift received at ordination." *Ratio Fundamentalis*, no. 81.

11　"This necessity [of ongoing formation] is intrinsic to the divine gift itself which is continually 'vivified' so the priest may adequately respond to his vocation. In fact, as a man situated in history, he needs to perfect himself in all the aspects of his human and spiritual existence in order to attain that conformity with Christ, the unifying principle of all things." DMLP, no. 87.

priestly life will be seen through the lens of a priest's Christian identity, his masculine identity, and his priestly identity. These three integral elements of his life together make up a holy, healthy priesthood.

17   Finally, good farmers want to identify anything that might hinder the growth of their crops, including imperfections in the soil and harmful factors in the environment. We address that topic in the latter half of this chapter, where we briefly consider some challenges facing priests in the United States today, such as shortcomings in priestly culture itself and harmful factors in the wider ecclesial and social environments. Although our intention is not to dwell on those obstacles or try to solve them, to acknowledge them is important. Becoming the kind of priest who can overcome those challenges is part of the very purpose of ongoing formation in the priesthood.

DESCRIPTION OF A HOLY, HEALTHY PRIESTHOOD
Christian Identity

18   The most defining choice we make in life is to have a relationship with Jesus, who draws us into communion with his Father through the love of the Holy Spirit. That relationship began with our baptismal rebirth, when we were claimed by Christ and incorporated into his Body, the Church. For most of us, our spiritual birth in baptism occurred in infancy, and we had as little choice in the matter as we did in our natural birth.

19   At some point, though—early in our childhood, perhaps a bit later in our teenage years, or maybe later still with a "second conversion" or reversion to the faith—we began to take personal responsibility for that relationship. We began to see the primacy of our friendship with Christ and took steps to deepen our interior life. Fostering that friendship with Jesus, so important for all Christians, is doubly

important for the priest who is called to be among the Lord's closest collaborators, to love the Church as the Lord does, and to stand in his very place in shepherding souls, proclaiming the Word of God, and administering the sacraments.

20 At the core of our Christian identity is recognizing our status as beloved sons of God. "See what love the Father has bestowed on us that we may be called the children of God. Yet so we are" (1 Jn 3:1). It is the very reason for the Incarnation. "The Son of God became the Son of man," St. Irenaeus wrote, so that "man . . . might become a son of God."[12] Taking our divine filiation seriously means assuming both its responsibilities and its privileges. As loyal sons we want to be in intimate contact with God through prayer and sacraments. We strive to obey the Father and his will, keep the moral law, care for our brothers and sisters, and guard ourselves against the Evil One, who constantly seeks to rob us of our dignity and diminish the fruitfulness of our ministry. The privileges of our sonship in Christ include a confident awareness of God's love and mercy, the gift of the Holy Spirit, the joy and peace of being in communion with the Father, and the assurance of salvation for those who die in a state of grace.

21 Like natural sonship, divine filiation is not something that we lose through sin. Even if we abandon the Father's house, we do not forfeit his love or our sonship. In the parable of the Prodigal Son, even after the young man's selfish betrayal, the good father remains vigilant, waiting for his son to return, ready to forgive and restore him to his rightful place in the family home. That is the image of our heavenly Father that Jesus gives us. When we stray, he waits in vigilance to

---

12   St. Irenaeus, *Adv. haeres.* 3, 19, 1: PG 7/1, 939, quoted in *Catechism of the Catholic Church*, 2nd ed. (Washington, DC: Libreria Editrice Vaticana–United States Conference of Catholic Bishops, 2016), no. 460. The *Catechism* is subsequently cited as CCC.

restore us to our rightful place in the family. When we do not resist such love, it draws out our own love and keeps alive our commitment to grow in holiness as sons of such a Father.

22 For priests, to be sons of God is to entrust ourselves under the provident care of the Father while striving to become a saint. Structuring the day around our interior growth, we beg for the grace to pursue the life of virtue, reject the temptation to settle for mediocrity, and wage battle against our evil inclinations. When weighed down by weakness or hurt by sin, we priests humbly confess our faults and joyfully return to the fight. Conforming our lives to that of Christ, we commit ourselves to daily prayer, personal sacrifice, and service to neighbor.[13]

23 As sons of God, we priests are also sons of the Church, faithful to it and grateful for its life-giving teachings. We honor and foster relationships with those brilliant examples of faith, the saintly sons and daughters of the Church through the ages. Priests nourish a special love for the Holy Mother of God[14] and for St. Joseph. "In this context the ecclesiology of communion becomes decisive for understanding the identity of the priest, his essential dignity, and his vocation and mission among the People of God and in the world. Reference to the Church is therefore necessary, even if not primary, in defining the identity of the priest. As a mystery, the Church is essentially related to Jesus Christ. She is his fullness, his body, his

---

13   "Therefore, the priest must necessarily live this relationship [with the Holy Trinity] in an intimate and personal manner, in dialogue of adoration and love with the three divine Persons, conscious that the gift has been received and has been given for the service of all." DMLP, no. 5.

14   "The priestly spirituality may not be considered complete if it does not take into serious consideration the testament of Christ crucified, when he willed to entrust his Mother to the beloved disciple, and through him to all the priests called to continue his work of redemption." DMLP, no. 84. See also CIC, c. 276 §2, 5°.

spouse. She is the 'sign' and living 'memorial' of his permanent presence and activity in our midst and on our behalf."[15]

24 Such are some features of our Christian identity. We priests hold them in common with all those who share the indescribable privilege of being children of God.

MASCULINE IDENTITY

25 Our identity as Christians is our greatest honor as priests. Yet this identity is not an abstract ideal. It depends upon and penetrates a prior reality, our human nature, which has a dignity all its own. In considering the elements of a holy and healthy priesthood, then, we must consider the characteristics of a fully human life. To be a thriving priest means to be a thriving man.

26 The Christian faith illuminates our humanity in important ways. It teaches, for example, that we find the highest human fulfillment in giving ourselves to the service of God and neighbor, that humility is the foundation of the virtuous life, and that our destiny lies beyond this world. As the Second Vatican Council taught, Christ "fully reveals man to man himself and makes his supreme calling clear."[16] For Christians, human nature flourishes to the extent that we conform our lives to the life and teachings of Jesus.

27 To be humanly mature as priests means that our personal development is free and integrated. We are *free* when we take responsibility for our own growth, when we pursue a life of virtue not under coercion but out of love. Our conscience is formed to perceive the good, and our will grows strong enough to pursue it. We are *integrated* when growth

---

15   PDV, no. 12.
16   Second Vatican Council, *Gaudium et Spes (Pastoral Constitution on the Church in the Modern World)*, no. 22, in *The Documents of Vatican II*, ed. Walter M. Abbott (New York: Corpus Books, 1966). Subsequently cited as GS.

is consistent in the various aspects of life—when we live a unity of life that does not compartmentalize and that achieves a "right balance of heart and mind, reason and feeling, body and soul."[17] Immaturity, for instance, may manifest itself in someone who is generous with strangers but selfish with friends, who devotes hours to prayer but neglects the basic duties of life, who is disciplined and tidy in professional work but lives in squalor, or who cultivates a polished public demeanor while privately disregarding his childish or eccentric manners.

28   An essential part of human maturity is affective maturity. The *Program of Priestly Formation* describes an affectively mature priest as "a man of feelings who is not driven by them but freely lives his life enriched by them."[18] This form of self-mastery makes genuine, selfless love possible. In particular, affective maturity is a precondition for the joyful embrace of chastity, the virtue that channels our capacity to love and enables us to love well. Although everyone is called to live chastely, the virtue assumes a special importance in the life of a priest called to celibacy.[19]

29   Our masculine identity is especially visible in our call to spiritual paternity. Like natural fathers, as spiritual fathers we should nurture human qualities that enable us to live this aspect of our vocation well: generosity, strength of character, kindness, patience, personal discipline, and courage, to name a few. The celibate priest should feel comfortable in his masculinity and possess rightly ordered sexual attractions. In addition, he should have the capacity and the desire for deep friendship, especially friendships with other priests, as well

---

17   DMLP, no. 93.
18   PPF, no. 183e.
19   Regarding married priests, see Benedict XVI, *Anglicanorum Coetibus (Apostolic Constitution Providing for Personal Ordinariates for Anglicans Entering into Full Communion with the Catholic Church)*, November 4, 2009, no. VI §2. See also Congregation for the Doctrine of the Faith, "Complementary Norms for the Apostolic Constitution *Anglicanorum Coetibus*," November 4, 2009, art. 6 §§1-2.

as the good judgment needed to maintain healthy friendships with both men and women.[20]

30 Finally, a thriving human life is one that keeps in balance the legitimate needs of both soul and body. Finding the time and energy to pray, to establish a healthy lifestyle, to get enough sleep, to exercise, and to relax without shirking our priestly duties demands prudence and discipline. We might not always get it right, but the mature individual always strives for that balance and rhythm.

PRIESTLY IDENTITY

31 Our masculine identity is given a specific direction through our Christian discipleship. Neither our faith nor our manhood can be understood in isolation from the other. The same can be said of our vocation as priests. The priesthood is not an isolated part of our lives; it is not merely our professional work or a set of pastoral responsibilities that we fulfill. The priesthood penetrates every aspect of our lives, touches every moment of our day, and gives purpose and meaning to our existence.

32 This is not to say that priests do not have a personal life with family and friends, interests and hobbies, and time away from pastoral work. To the contrary, as mentioned above, such components of a healthy life contribute to a thriving priesthood. At the same time, we became priests knowing that the priesthood is a vocation that would demand much of us. A priest does not belong entirely to himself; he has given himself in a radical and sacrificial way to be "anxious about the things of the Lord, how he may please the Lord" (1 Cor 7:32). This self-giving is the pastoral charity of the priest.[21] It is intrinsic to

---

20   PPF, nos. 187g and 186. See CIC, c. 277 §2.
21   "Pastoral charity is the virtue by which we imitate Christ in his self-giving and service. It is not just what we do, but our gift of self, which manifests Christ's love for his flock. Pastoral charity determines

the logic of his priesthood. It flows from his configuration to Christ the Head and Shepherd, by which he participates in Jesus' pastoral charity. The essential content of this pastoral charity is the total gift of self to the Church, following the example of Christ. When a priest accepts the call to Holy Orders, he also accepts the vocation to offer himself for the sake of others. Struggles in the priesthood often begin when that freely chosen, personal sacrifice is later scaled down in favor of personal comforts and a life of ease.

33   A joyful spirit of sacrifice and self-giving therefore lies at the heart of our priestly identity. When a man becomes a natural father, his heart expands to embrace his new child in such a way that the sacrifices he must now make become easy. Such is the normal course of fatherhood, and it is no different for us as spiritual fathers. "Unless you 'exit' from yourself," Pope Francis said in his 2014 Chrism Mass homily, "the oil grows rancid and the anointing cannot be fruitful." However, if the priest does "exit" from himself, the pope said, "Your people will make you feel and taste who you are, what your name is, what your identity is, and they will make you rejoice in that hundredfold which the Lord has promised to those who serve him."[22] A father who gladly sacrifices for his children is both a good father and a joyful one. The priest and the natural father understand that their leadership role is only truly expressed in radical service. A priest who does not count the cost, who resists the temptation to chip away at his radical gift of self, who willingly gives away even his personal time when necessary, will be both a good spiritual father and a joyful one—and eventually a holy one.

---

our way of thinking and acting, our way of relating to people. It makes special demands on us." PDV, no. 23.

22   Francis, Homily, 2014 Chrism Mass, April 17, 2014.

34 The capacity for spiritual fatherhood is a useful lens through which to gauge other dimensions of our priestly identity. For instance, a father is committed to the growth of his children and wishes to see them thrive, even to surpass him in excellence. A fatherly priest, too, will desire the best for those entrusted to his care and will earnestly promote their spiritual growth—rejoicing when they surpass him even in holiness. A priest living pastoral charity has a zeal for the salvation of souls and generously gives himself to all, particularly those most in need of his care: the poor, the sick, the elderly, the lonely, the abandoned, and the outcast.[23]

35 As a good husband is faithful to his wife, the priest fosters in his heart a deep, spousal love for the Church and fidelity to its teachings. The "priest's life ought to radiate this spousal character," as Pope St. John Paul II wrote in *Pastores Dabo Vobis*, "which demands that he be a witness to Christ's spousal love and thus be capable of loving people with a heart which is new, generous and pure."[24] He will be eager to administer the sacraments: washing souls in the regenerating waters of Baptism, healing them in Penance and Reconciliation and in the Anointing of the Sick, and uniting Christian couples in the sacrament of Holy Matrimony. He will rejoice particularly in providing his spiritual sons and daughters with the spiritual nourishment found in the Eucharist, the "source and summit" of our faith and indeed of his priesthood.[25]

---

23 "The Lord will say this clearly: his anointing is meant for the poor, prisoners and the sick, for those who are sorrowing and alone. My dear brothers, the ointment is not intended just to make us fragrant, much less to be kept in a jar, for then it would become rancid . . . and the heart bitter." Francis, Homily, 2013 Chrism Mass.
24 PDV, no. 22.
25 See Second Vatican Council, *Lumen Gentium (Dogmatic Constitution on the Church)*, no. 11, in *The Documents of Vatican II*, ed. Walter M. Abbott (New York: Corpus Books, 1966). Subsequently cited as LG. "In fact, there is an intimate connection among the centrality of the Eucharist, pastoral charity and the unity of the life of the priest, who therein finds decisive indications for the way to holiness to which he has been specifically called." DMLP, no. 66.

36   A holy and healthy priest will find his happiness in humble service, seeking not "to be served but to serve" (Mt 20:28). He recognizes in the people he serves the talents meant to build up the Body of Christ, and he promotes the proper autonomy of the lay vocation: to "seek the kingdom of God by engaging in temporal affairs and by ordering them according to the plan of God."[26] He will find repugnant any semblance of a clericalist mindset that lords authority over his people,[27] or even its subtler manifestation that seeks to "clericalize the laity" by reducing the dignity of their vocation to official church organizations or roles in the Sacred Liturgy. He will readily collaborate with all the baptized, recognizing their genuine and vital participation in the mission of the Church.[28]

37   In the image of the priest's anointing (quoted in paragraph 33), Pope Francis points to a beautiful truth about the nature of pastoral charity and maturation in priestly ministry. There is a wonderful reciprocal relation between the priest and his people that leads to mutual human and spiritual growth.[29] Pope Francis speaks of a generous humble priest coming to "feel and taste" his full identity as a priest through his relationship with his people. A priest who is open to the dignity and gifts of his people and willing to enter into communion with them in their faith, hope, trials, and joys will be formed by them. He

---

26   LG, no. 31.
27   "The specificity of the ministerial priesthood, however, is defined not on the basis of its supposed 'superiority' over the common priesthood, but rather by the service it is called to carry out for all the faithful so they may adhere to the mediation and Lordship of Christ rendered visible by the exercise of the ministerial priesthood." DMLP, no. 6.
28   See CIC, c. 275 §2.
29   St. John Paul II asserts a similar point when he speaks of communion between the priest and his people as formative: "Those responsible for the ongoing formation of priests are to be found in the Church as 'communion.' In this sense, the entire particular church has the responsibility, under the guidance of the bishop, to develop and look after the different aspects of her priests' permanent formation. Priests are not there to serve themselves but the People of God. So, ongoing formation, in ensuring the human, spiritual, intellectual and pastoral maturity of priests, is doing good to the People of God itself. Besides, the very exercise of the pastoral ministry leads to a constant and fruitful mutual exchange between the priest's life of faith and that of the laity. Indeed the very relationship and sharing of life between the priest and the community, if it is wisely conducted and made use of, will be a fundamental contribution to permanent formation, which cannot be reduced to isolated episodes or initiatives, but covers the whole ministry and life of the priest." PDV, no. 78.

embraces the beauty and value of the co-responsibility of all baptized in building the Kingdom. Even as he helps his people grow through his ministry, his people will help him become a better minister of God's grace and mercy. The priest will benefit from his people's wisdom and insights to grow in understanding. The goodness and holiness of his people can inspire him to seek a deeper union with his Savior. Their struggles and heartaches will move him to have recourse to intercession and teach him to preach a word that will comfort and renew hope. The various difficulties of his people will lead him to seek practical means to assist. For example, the pastor of an immigrant community may need to help his people with medical and legal aid or adult education. These are not things most priests are trained to do, but with generous hearts they will grow in order to serve their people. In these ways, the community will draw him into greater pastoral charity and help form in the priest a deeper identity as spouse and father that will inspire and enliven "his daily existence, enriching it with gifts and demands, virtues and incentives."[30]

38   To flourish, a priest will take great care to fulfill the promises that he made on the day of his ordination. He will see his celibate commitment as a path to undivided love for God and for his people, a living witness to supernatural realities, a fitting complement to his spousal love for the Church, and a privileged way of living spiritual fatherhood. His obedience to the Church, and specifically to his diocesan bishop and the Holy Father, will be mature, free, and ungrudging.[31] Praying for the Church and especially for those entrusted to his ministry, through the Liturgy of the Hours and his

---

30   PDV, no. 27.

31   "By its very nature, the ordained ministry can be carried out only to the extent that the priest is united to Christ through sacramental participation in the priestly order, and thus to the extent that he is in hierarchical communion with his own bishop. The ordained ministry has a radical 'communitarian form' and can only be carried out as 'a collective work' (Angelus, Feb. 25, 1990)." PDV, no. 17. See also CIC, c. 273.

own personal prayer, will be a steadfast, daily resolution.[32] Last, his promise to live a simple life will be more than an aspiration; he will make choices about his lifestyle, his home, his car, his meals, his entertainment, his vacations, and his hobbies that reflect the sobriety of a man committed entirely to the Lord.[33] He will "use such goods with a sense of responsibility, moderation, upright intention and detachment proper to him who has his treasure in heaven."[34]

39 "Moreover, all [priests] are required to make a sincere effort to live in mutual esteem, to respect others and to hold in esteem all the positive and legitimate diversities present in the presbyterate. This too constitutes part of the priest's spiritual life and continual practice of asceticism." In addition, "priests who belong to religious orders and congregations represent a spiritual enrichment for the entire diocesan presbyterate, to which they contribute specific charisms and special ministries, stimulating the particular church by their presence to be more intensely open to the Church throughout the world."[35] This effort includes the common life that diocesan priests share in a rectory or that religious priests share in community. Priests who live together should recognize divine providence in this arrangement, not merely circumstance by chance.

Dedication to a Life of Learning and Growing

40 Overarching these three identities of a priest is an attitude to life that is crucial for his ongoing formation. No matter how long or fruitful his formation in seminary, a priest's growth does not end on the day of his ordination. St. Gregory of Nazianzen said that "extreme old age would not be a long preparation for the priesthood."[36] We always

---

32   See CIC, c. 276 §2, 3° and 5°.
33   See CIC, c. 282 §1.
34   DMLP, no. 83.
35   PDV, no. 31.
36   St. Gregory Nazianzen, Oration 2, no. 72.

have more to discover and more ways to progress personally and in our priestly ministry.[37] Changes in life demand that we be prepared to continue adapting to new circumstances. We have a need, then, for constant dedication to learning and growth.

41 Without a humble acknowledgment of our shortcomings, we will find it impossible to embrace an attitude that is receptive to true, ongoing formation. A mature and responsible priest is attentive to the gaps in his formation and flaws in his character. He takes the initiative to address them. When they are pointed out by others—whether family members, friends, the people he serves, fellow collaborators in the vineyard, or his brother priests or bishop—he responds with gratitude. In fact, he invites such feedback, especially from his priest friends and from his mentors, particularly his spiritual director. In this way, he makes himself accountable to others and opens paths for ongoing growth in all areas of his life.

42 Each priest is an individual. One of the purposes of this document is to survey the landscape of ongoing formation in order to assist a priest in assessing his own formation needs. It may be that his interior life has grown cold and superficial, or that his intellectual life has atrophied since his more studious days in the seminary. Perhaps his pastoral ministry has ceased being a source of joy and renewal. He might wish to rekindle his battle against certain temptations. Maybe the priest realizes his need for better interpersonal or listening skills, for more detachment from devices and digital media, or for more authentic friendships. He may need to make a renewed effort to reach out to those on the peripheries, such as the poor, migrants, and refugees. Whatever his formation needs are, he will want to make a deep examination that will require self-knowledge, the courage to

---

37   See CIC, c. 279, §§1-3.

change, and openness to healing and grace. These, too, are essential elements of a priest's self-identity if he is to build a habit of ongoing formation.

43 Committing ourselves to ongoing formation can be arduous. It would be easier simply to coast through our priesthood without ever challenging ourselves to keep growing. But living organisms that do not grow do not produce. This undertaking, difficult as it may be, is a means to flourish as a priest, as a Christian, and as a man. It is the road where we will continually meet the Lord, ever eager for our true good, and hence it is the way to genuine joy.

CHALLENGES TO LIVING THE PRIESTHOOD TODAY

44 The qualities of a holy, healthy priesthood explored in the preceding paragraphs constitute the goal of ongoing formation, the ultimate fruit of the divine Farmer's labor. Although none but the Lord ever attained the perfection of life represented in all these qualities, with the assurance of grace we can continue pressing onward toward their fulfillment in our lives, however imperfect the result may be.

45 Nevertheless, in addition to this goal, we must consider those obstacles that can choke the seed from growing properly. Every priest encounters some of these difficulties. The purpose of this document is not to give specific instructions to resolve them, but rather to encourage priests to live the kind of lives that can best meet them. The descriptions of these obstacles, then, are intentionally cursory. They offer just a glimpse, but they are an important acknowledgment of the kinds of challenges that any personal plan of ongoing formation should address.

46   As observed earlier, these obstacles come in the form of imperfections in the priestly culture itself as well as harmful factors in both the ecclesial and the wider social environment. This section groups these shortcomings under these three, admittedly overlapping, general subheadings: within the priesthood, within the Church, and from the wider culture.

WITHIN THE PRIESTHOOD

47   Many of the challenges we face are of a more personal nature. For instance, an increasing number of priests struggle with the repercussions of unhealthy family dynamics in their upbringing. Many come from broken or dysfunctional families that have left them fragile, lacking in confidence, distrustful of authority, and sometimes in need of spiritual and psychological healing. These wounds are often compounded by the danger of isolation in a cultural environment that tends to prioritize individualism above all else. The rich tapestry of parochial relationships that once supported priests, often including life in common among priests themselves, is now greatly diminished. As a consequence, many priests experience their celibacy primarily as loneliness, as a difficult sacrifice, and not as a gift intended to expand the heart with a broad and profound love for God and neighbor.

48   Clergy shortages and aging presbyterates have contributed to higher workloads and stress levels among almost all priests. Many young priests are appointed pastor of one or more parishes shortly after ordination, causing them to feel underprepared and overwhelmed and to feel they have been left to fend for themselves. The mounting workload often leads to a frenetic focus on activity and pastoral

work, an activism that can drain one's desire for spiritual intimacy with God and promote superficiality in the interior life.[38]

49 Feeling trapped by an expectation of work that can never be accomplished, many priests fail to care for their souls and even for their natural well-being, neglecting sleep, health, and relationships. Authentic fraternity among priests, like all friendships, requires a commitment of time and energy; in light of their workloads, many priests are reluctant to make that commitment. Many lack life-giving relationships among family members and friends, further isolating them. All too often, priests seek to fill the void left by these relationships using virtual relationships instead, through an unhealthy, sometimes even sinful, use of social media and other Internet resources. As occurs in the wider culture, priests find their growing reliance on "digital friends" to be depressing and unfulfilling.

50 For some priests, personal isolation is intensified still more by an overly clerical understanding of the priesthood. By clericalism we mean not a proper understanding of legitimate priestly authority, still less a healthy love for the clerical vocation. Rather, clericalism is a fixation on one's status as a priest, an eager demand for respect, and an implied superiority over others. Ultimately it means that a priest has forgotten that he is first a disciple, in common with all other Christians, and that his glory is to be a son of God. His priestly vocation is an invitation into a deep friendship with Christ so that he can more fruitfully serve his brothers and sisters and indeed the whole world. By embracing the flawed attitude of the Apostles, who argued over who was the greatest (see Lk 9:46, 22:24, and so on),

---

38 "Due to numerous duties stemming in large part from pastoral activity, the priest's life is now linked more so than ever before to a series of requests that could lead him to mounting *activism*, making him subject to a pace at times overwhelming and frenetic. Not to be forgotten against this temptation is the first intention of Jesus, which was to call to his side Apostles so they "would remain with him" (Mk 3:14)." DMLP, no. 51 (emphasis original).

clericalism fosters division within the Church and further isolates priests from the very people who should be among the primary supporters of their vocation.

51 Finally, many priests unfortunately face these struggles apart from any awareness of the supernatural. The Lord permits us to encounter setbacks, weaknesses, even persecution, but he never asks us to shoulder more than he gives us the grace to bear. Seeing things, including struggles, from a supernatural point of view offers a perspective that brings confidence, peace, and even joy in the midst of difficulties. When a priest is overwhelmed by obstacles in his life and ministry, it may be that he has forgotten in whom his strength rests.[39] "If the priest does not count on the primacy of grace," the 2013 DMLP observes, "he will not be able to respond to the challenges of his times, and any pastoral program is destined to failure, no matter how elaborate it may be."[40] Recovering an abiding sense of supernatural joy and trust, then, will be among our first priorities in confronting the challenges we face.

WITHIN THE CHURCH

52 Other difficulties confronting the priest emerge from the situation of the Church in many parts of the United States today. In many parts of the country, for instance, an understandable sense of demoralization has been caused by certain trends in the Church. These include a steep decline in Mass attendance, the widespread closing of parishes and schools, and a general sense of decline. Priests are not alone in lamenting these trends, of course, but we are often affected in a deeper and more personal way. At the same time, the Church is growing in other areas of the country. The priests in those areas can

---

39 "The LORD is my shepherd; / there is nothing I lack" (Ps 23:1). "I have the strength for everything through him who empowers me" (Phil 4:13).

40 DMLP, introduction to chap. 2.

be challenged to meet the needs of the increasing population with fewer priests than required, and with staff and volunteers who are making heroic efforts to help and lead in the Church but who are also limited by their family and work responsibilities.

53   In addition, some priests and people are frustrated and demoralized by the impact of the sexual abuse scandals that seem never to go away. Many priests feel that they are laboring under a perpetual shadow of suspicion, cast not only by wider society but by their own people, who are affected by the relentless media stories on clergy malfeasance. Many priests, too, worry that their diocesan bishops will not support them in the event of an accusation. Also, priests sometimes fear that, if accused, they will not be afforded the presumption of innocence prescribed by canon law[41] and central to the US legal system as well.

54   An atmosphere that can be perceived as divisive can be inflamed by an erosion of ecclesial and fraternal communion. Deep theological and liturgical differences often can be found among priests of different age groups, differences that impede cross-generational fraternity. This division is exacerbated by overwrought websites, of both the progressive and traditionalist variety, that present themselves as a kind of "parallel Magisterium" purporting to be more reliable than the actual Magisterium of the Church. Furthermore, as in every age, clerical envy and comparisons continue to diminish the unity that we should enjoy as brother priests.

From the Wider Culture

55   Then we must consider the obstacles that arise from the wider US culture. Social divisions, of course, have always been part of our diverse society. Today, however, they seem to have reached a new

---

41   See CIC, c. 1321.

intensity. Racism and old nativist bigotries continue to foster injustice and fray the solidarity of our society. New prejudices against people of faith or moral conviction have added to this disorder. Political ideologies are intensifying, and their core constituencies are drifting further and further apart. The worldviews of opposing camps are increasingly at odds, even incompatible. Moral bonds once forged by a common outlook seem to be disintegrating. Tensions are rising, and few in our country seem able to have sober discussions. This atmosphere of bitter antagonism has seeped into the Church and even into the priesthood. It does not make the pursuit of holiness any easier for our priests, who themselves are sometimes swept into a highly emotivist approach to resolving conflict.

56 A final, but by no means inconsequential, source of pressure on priests comes from our highly secularized society. We can easily identify bright lines of disagreement between the Church's doctrine and the increasingly intolerant doctrines of secular ideals, starting with the strident rejection of the right to life of the unborn. This core tenet of the secularist creed will inevitably start to include—indeed has already started to do so—other vulnerable populations such as the elderly and the terminally ill. Other elements of our society just as strongly oppose any openness to migrants and refugees. Priests and faithful Catholics will continue, at great personal cost, to work at the forefront of the campaign to protect the rights of those who otherwise have no voice in society.

57 This secularist outlook has also championed a view of the human person and human sexuality that directly opposes the Christian point of view. In the 1960s the sexual revolution detached sexual behavior from traditional social and religious norms. It then evolved into the acceptance, even celebration, of ever more deviant sexual behavior.

Society has now gone so far as to obstinately deny even basic biological realities. Catholics find themselves ever more disenfranchised from the secular mainstream. Aggressive homosexual and transgender ideologies seek—through social pressure, soft intimidation, and even the force of law—to silence the Church. As priests we feel that pressure in a particular way, especially as we are called to minister to all people in mercy and yet also in truth.

58   The secular revolution seems unstoppable and can be disheartening. Anti-Christian narratives of history are being taught unapologetically and uncritically to our children. Sexual instruction in public and some private schools often strives to indoctrinate children early and forcefully in the secular and deceiving view of the human person and human sexuality. In its attempts to propose an alternative, the Church finds itself at an extreme disadvantage. It has lost much credibility, in part due to the sexual abuse scandals, and is now hemmed in by mounting restrictions on religious freedom and engagement in the public square.

59   The situation seems bleak, especially if we priests are not finding strength and consolation in our union with God. A priest who lacks deep roots can easily be carried away by any—let alone all—of these obstacles. Building strong foundations of a holy, healthy priesthood is ever more necessary if we are to respond to these obstacles with confidence, peace, and joy. This document proposes a way of life that will make it possible.

CHAPTER TWO
Ongoing Formation

60   After his Resurrection, Jesus spent forty days with his disciples before he ascended into heaven. The Scriptures reveal little about those days, but we know that they were a time of more intense formation for the newly ordained priests, with Jesus "appearing to them . . . and speaking about the kingdom of God" (Acts 1:3).

61   What sort of things did they talk about? On the road to Emmaus, Jesus unpacked the biblical law and prophecies to two disciples and showed them how the "Messiah should suffer these things and enter into his glory." Luke goes on to tell us that, "beginning with Moses and all the prophets, he interpreted to them what referred to him in all the scriptures" (24:26-27). What Jesus said to those two disciples, he surely would have said to his Apostles, perhaps adding that they too would have to undergo many sufferings in carrying out their pastoral mission. Jesus would have led his newly ordained priests in prayer and perhaps outlined features of the Church that would come fully alive on the day of Pentecost, features to which they would devote their lives. That period of intense preparation, initiated by Jesus himself, is a precedent for ongoing formation in the priesthood.

62   This present document proposes a way of life that enables priests to stay on the path of continual growth so as to remain with Jesus after ordination as he continues to form them for the ministry. Chapter one sketched an image of a holy, healthy priesthood and pointed out some obstacles to its development. This second chapter examines some principles of effective ongoing formation and suggests ways to act on those principles.

63   There is much at stake. St. Faustina wrote in her diary, "O Jesus, give us fervent and holy priests! Oh, how great is the dignity of the priest, but at the same time, how great is his responsibility! Much has been given you, O priest, but much will also be demanded of you."[42] The responsibility is great, and the demands are great. But we do not carry these burdens alone. This chapter surveys some ways for a priest to receive help to become the priest he is meant to be.

FORMATION IS A LIFELONG PROCESS

GROWTH IS A SIGN OF LIFE

64   Every one of us began our priestly formation in childhood. Ideally, a boy destined for the priesthood is born into a loving and intact family, learns the rudiments of his faith along with his elementary education, and enjoys a formation in virtue and self-control from his earliest years. The Second Vatican Council called the family the "first seminary,"[43] because his childhood home is where the future priest begins the personal and spiritual formation that will become the foundation of his vocation. None of us, of course, was raised in a perfect family; many suffer the lingering effects of a family life that was far from the ideal. Nevertheless, whatever its strengths and weaknesses, our family provided the impetus for our initial growth, and it is to our family, especially our parents, that we owe much of our vocation.[44]

---

42   St. Faustina, *Diary of Saint Maria Faustina Kowalska: Divine Mercy in My Soul* (Stockbridge, MA: Marian Press, 2005), no. 941.

43   Second Vatican Council, *Optatam Totius (Decree on the Training of Priests)*, no. 2, in *Vatican Council II: Volume 1. The Conciliar and Post Conciliar Documents*, new rev. ed., ed. Austin Flannery (Northport, NY: Costello, 1996). Subsequently cited as OT.

44   "The Church is called to cooperate with parents though suitable pastoral initiatives, assisting them in the fulfillment of their educational mission. She must always do this by helping them to appreciate their proper role and to realize that by their reception of the sacrament of marriage they become ministers of their children's education. In educating them, they build up the Church, and in so doing, they accept a God-given vocation." Francis, *Amoris Laetitia (On Love in the Family)* (Vatican City: Vatican Press, 2016), no. 85. See CIC, cc. 226, 233 §1, 793, and 1136.

65　By the time we entered our teenage years, we started to discover our own personality, talents, and weaknesses. We began to differentiate ourselves and were molded by our interests, the influence of our friends, and increasingly, the pressures of social media. Graduating from high school was a significant milestone, but we soon realized that our growth was not complete. We continued to be stretched by continuing our education or starting a career; we acquired more skills, built new friendships, and expanded our horizons. That forward momentum is part of thriving. If humans are not personally challenged, life becomes tedious and flat. Those who have fallen into a rut know the heavy weight of stagnation. Growth, in short, is the dynamic of any healthy life.

66　This dynamic is as true in the life of priests as it is in the life of all. When we entered the seminary, we did so with the understanding that we needed several years of preparation before we would be ready for the priesthood. We received formation in the human, spiritual, intellectual, and pastoral dimensions. Eventually we came to our ordination, and our lives changed dramatically when we began our ministry. Yet ordination was not the end of our formation, any more than high school or college was.

Post-Seminary Formation

67　Growth is a mark of a healthy priesthood. Many spiritual writers have commented that the interior life never stands still. It is like walking uphill on a gravel path. Either we move forward or slip backward. The priesthood, too, is a dynamic reality that, like the interior life, cannot simply stand still. We are always either advancing or backsliding. Ongoing formation proposes a set of guidelines and resources to help us keep growing. It ensures that changes in our life, which are inevitable, are directed well and contribute to our continued flourishing as men and as priests. Ongoing formation continues the work that began in our seminary years. "This journey," the *Ratio Fundamentalis* states, "is the natural continuation of the process of building up priestly identity begun in Seminary and accomplished sacramentally in priestly ordination, in view of a pastoral service that causes it to mature over time."[45] This *Guide*, in fact, can be seen as a sequel to the *Program of Priestly Formation*, which was first published in 1971 and is now in its sixth edition.[46]

68 Ongoing formation is needed to address not only the normal life changes that affect every priest but also the limitations of seminary formation. In some surveys, recently ordained priests have identified gaps in their formation.[47] Some of those concerns are well-founded critiques of seminary programs that rightly point out areas for improvement. Others, however, reveal not so much gaps in seminary formation as the need for further formation. After all, many aspects of priestly life—administrative abilities, financial expertise, leadership, and certain pastoral skills, to take some clear examples—are only fully learned in the field. Rather than shoehorning these important skills into an already burdened seminary curriculum—likely with dubious results—it seems wiser for the Church to provide some basics about these topics during the seminary years while actively fostering their development after ordination.[48]

---

45 *Ratio Fundamentalis*, no. 81. "It is particularly important to be aware of and to respect the intrinsic link between formation before ordination to the priesthood and formation after ordination. Should there be a break in continuity, or worse a complete difference between these two phases of formation, there would be serious and immediate repercussions on pastoral work and fraternal communion among priests, especially those in different age groups." PDV, no. 71.

46 "Ongoing formation is not a repetition of the formation acquired in the seminary, simply reviewed or expanded with new and practical suggestions. Ongoing formation involves relatively new content and especially methods; it develops as a harmonious and vital process which—rooted in the formation received in the seminary—calls for adaptations, updating and modifications, but without sharp breaks in continuity." PDV, no. 71.

47 See National Association of Catholic Theological Schools and Center for Applied Research in the Apostolate (CARA), *Enter by the Narrow Gate: Satisfaction and Challenges Among Recently Ordained Priests* (Washington, DC: CARA, 2020).

48 "Initial and ongoing formation are distinct because each requires different methods and timing, but they are two halves of one reality, the life of a disciple cleric, in love with his Lord and steadfastly

69 Just as the integration of the four dimensions is vital in seminarians, ongoing formation strives to continue integrating the dimensions in priests. Each of the dimensions deserves our attention. If four rowers are pulling a boat, each needs to pull with equal force, or the boat makes little progress. Just so, if we focus exclusively on our continued spiritual development but ignore our pastoral growth, for instance, we risk becoming spiritual recluses and absentee fathers. If we focus on our pastoral work but ignore intellectual pursuits, our preaching and teaching can become superficial and stale. If we focus on academic studies but ignore the need for greater human maturity, we can become eccentric and off-putting. Each priest will want to tailor his personal plan for ongoing formation to meet his own needs, addressing his own weaknesses and building on his own strengths, without ever losing sight of his whole person.

MEANS FOR ONGOING FORMATION

70 This *Guide* addresses each dimension of formation in its own chapter (chapters three through six), beginning with some objective markers in the life of a priest that reflect that chapter's dimension. The markers of human formation, for example, are fruits that we should expect in our lives when we apply ourselves to growing in human maturity and virtue. After summarizing these markers, each chapter then considers specific approaches to ongoing formation that may be helpful for priests. These means of formation fall under three headings: personal, fraternal, and episcopal. When engaging these means, which are discussed in this section, we are always aware that they are occasions to avail ourselves of the accompaniment of the Holy Spirit, who is our primary formator.[49]

following him." Francis, Address to the Plenary of the Congregation for the Clergy, October 3, 2014.
49   See DMLP, nos. 9-12.

Personal Means

71 The personal means of formation are the individual practices and attitudes that promote ongoing growth, because the priest remains "principally and primarily responsible for his own ongoing formation."[50] In most cases, these personal means are simply the extension of habits that we first nurtured in the seminary. A good starting point for many priests who wish to deepen their formation is therefore a return to the basics that began in the seminary: recovering the fervor that animated their lives prior to ordination. Many seasoned priests can witness to this beautiful experience of a "second conversion" that has breathed new vitality into their priestly lives and ministry.[51] The personal means of formation, if taken seriously, have a unique potential to return a priest to the first love that inspired his vocation at the very beginning.

72 The point of departure for the personal means of ongoing formation is the priest's own investment in the undertaking. As in our seminary years, we remain the primary agent of our formation. However good our seminary might have been, it could only make us into holy and effective priests if we applied ourselves to what we learned and assimilated it into our lives.[52] So too in ongoing formation, the best resources in the world will do little to help a priest who does not make the effort to grow. It is up to us to make formation a priority, by giving it the time, attention, and energy that it deserves.[53]

---

50 *Ratio Fundamentalis*, no. 82. "The term 'ongoing formation' is a reminder that the one experience of discipleship of those called to priesthood is never interrupted. The priest not only 'learns to know Christ' but, under the action of the Holy Spirit, he finds himself within a process of gradual and continuous configuration to Him, in his being and his acting, which constantly challenges the person to inner growth." *Ratio Fundamentalis*, no. 80.

51 "Ongoing formation is intended to ensure fidelity to the priestly ministry in a continuing journey of conversion, in order to rekindle the gift received at ordination." *Ratio Fundamentalis*, no. 81.

52 "This necessity [for ongoing formation] is intrinsic to the divine gift itself which is to be continually 'vivified' so the priest may adequately respond to his vocation. In fact, as a man situated in history, he needs to perfect himself in all the aspects of his human and spiritual existence in order to attain that conformity with Christ, the unifying principle of all things." DMLP, no. 87.

53 "Ongoing formation is a right-duty of the priest and imparting it is a right-duty of the Church. It is therefore stipulated in universal law." DMLP, no. 90; see CIC, c. 279.

73   In St. Peter's Basilica, a mosaic of Ananias and Sapphira faces the priest who emerges from the sacristy to celebrate Mass. These two early disciples were found wanting because they sold their land but secretly withheld a portion of their proceeds from the Apostles. They wanted to create the impression that they had given all their revenue, without actually having done so. It is no coincidence that the mosaic greets the priest in St. Peter's Basilica as he walks to the altar for the most important moment of his day.

74   Too often, we priests may give the impression of having made a complete gift of ourselves, while we hold back the time and energy that rightfully belong to God. Taking our ongoing formation seriously is a way of keeping our priesthood rooted in pastoral charity. It helps us continue to give ourselves generously to God and to his people. If we devote ourselves to personal growth in the priesthood, we can be sure that the Holy Spirit will multiply our efforts and forge us into the priests we dreamed of becoming on the day of our ordination.[54]

FRATERNAL MEANS

75   When our Lord commissioned his disciples to preach the Kingdom of God, he sent them out two by two. He could have doubled his reach in those first efforts to preach the Gospel by sending them out singly, but he knew that their mutual support would more than compensate for the loss. The book of Proverbs teaches that "a brother that is helped by his brother is like a strong city" (18:19, translated from the Vulgate). The Church herself reflects this emphasis on solidarity in its visible

---

54   "Precisely for this reason, it [that is, ongoing formation] cannot be a limited task, because priests never stop being disciples of Jesus, who follow Him. Sometimes we proceed with celerity, at other times our step is hesitant, we stop and we may even fall, but always staying on the path. Therefore, formation understood as discipleship accompanies the ordained minister his entire life and regards his person as a whole, intellectually, humanly and spiritually." Francis, Address to the Plenary of the Congregation for the Clergy, October 3, 2014.

structure, its bonds of charity, and its life of prayer. Our Catholic faith is a family affair, not a solitary path to individual enlightenment.[55]

76   What is true of the faith in general is true of a priest's life. Our life is intimately bound up with the lives of our brothers in the priesthood. Friendships forged in the seminary and after ordination reflect the natural bonds of companionship that should enrich every human life. "Life is stronger than death," Pope Francis taught in *Fratelli Tutti*, "when it is built on true relationships and bonds of fidelity. On the contrary, there is no life when we claim to be self-sufficient and live as islands: in these attitudes, death prevails."[56] In the priesthood, however, these friendships have the potential to be a great deal more. United by a common faith, outlook on life, commitment to virtue, and mission in the world, brother priests understand and can support each other in a unique way.[57] At the heart of priestly fraternity is the common bond of men seeking to follow Christ as his priests and committing to support one another on the path. When we rely on each other to travel this sometimes arduous road, we forge friendships of mutual respect, trust, and affection; in these friendships, openness about our struggles is possible. While not all priests in a presbyterate can have deep friendships with each other, they should be always aware that they are called to a friendship with their brothers characterized by a fraternal spirit of kindness, welcome, and openness to relationship. This is true of priests of all ages and

---

55   "Unity among the priests with the Bishop and among themselves is not something added from the outside to the nature of their service, but expresses its essence inasmuch as it is the care of Christ the priest for the people gathered in the unity of the Blessed Trinity." PDV, no. 74.

      "By its very nature, the ordained ministry can be carried out only to the extent that the priest is united to Christ through sacramental participation in the priestly order, and thus to the extent that he is in hierarchical communion with his own bishop. The ordained ministry has a radical 'communitarian form' and can only be carried out as 'a collective work.'" PDV, no. 17.

56   Francis, *Fratelli Tutti (On Fraternity and Social Friendship)*, October 3, 2020, no. 87.

57   "Priestly fraternity is the first setting in which ongoing formation takes place." *Ratio Fundamentalis*, no. 82.

perspectives. All priests share particular brotherhood in Christ and should relate to each other in accord with this familial identity.

77 If we are grappling with challenges in our ministry, for instance, another priest often can offer us the best advice. If our hearts are full of gratitude for the conversion of a parishioner, another priest can share that joy most deeply. If we feel the pain of rejection when we preach the Gospel, a priest can best encourage us. If we are experiencing the ache of celibacy with greater intensity, a brother priest who has walked the same road can offer the most reliable support and guidance. If we need to be corrected, if we are ever treading dangerous ground, if we are slipping in our priestly duties or developing unwholesome habits, or if we are crossing boundaries in our relationships—it is almost always another priest who can best see what is happening and lead us back. Healthy priests are able to both receive and offer fraternal correction; they are also able to offer and accept praise. Other friendships are important, even essential, in our lives, but they are never equivalent to our friendships with priests.

78 Certainly, priestly fraternity has limitations. It is not a panacea for every ill. If we do not make the effort to form and sustain friendships, they will not be there to help us. If we are insincere and hide the reality of our lives from our friends, they will be unable to advise us. Neither are priest friendships, even at their best, an emotional replacement for the sacrifice of marriage and the affections of a family. That is a sacrifice which, at some level, we each must bear—just as, when the sacrifice is well-lived, we each experience its particular joys.

79 When our friendships are deep and genuine, though, they are an incomparable source of happiness and an integral part of our ongoing formation as men and as priests. They are "a source of serenity and

joy in the exercise of the ministry," the DMLP states: "a decisive form of support in difficulties, and valuable help for growth in the pastoral charity which the priest must exercise in a particular way toward those confreres in difficulty and in need of understanding, assistance and support."[58] This can include simple, unstructured time together; small groups, such as those following the Jesus Caritas model; theological or book discussion groups;[59] or established associations of priests.[60]

80   New models of common priestly life are advancing as well. In areas where many parishes are served by single priests (that is, priests living alone in their parishes), they may be able to live in a single rectory and enjoy the benefits of common life without detracting from their individual service to their parishes.[61] Some priests, with the permission of their diocesan bishop, live under a formal rule of life while jointly serving a variety of apostolates assigned by their diocese.[62] Whether or not these options are available, priests in a

---

58   DMLP, no. 37.

59   *"Fraternal meetings:* some priests organize *fraternal meetings* for prayer, perhaps by reading the Word of God together in the form of *Lectio Divina*, developing their understanding of some theological or pastoral theme, sharing a ministerial endeavor, helping one another or simply spending some time together. These meetings in their various forms are the simplest and most common expression of priestly fraternity. In any case, it is strongly desirable to promote them." *Ratio Fundamentalis*, no. 88 (emphasis original).

60   "Its diverse modalities are to be encouraged according to possibilities and practical conditions, without necessarily transferring the albeit praiseworthy models proper to the religious life. Worthy of praise in particular are those associations which support priestly fraternity, holiness in the exercise of the ministry, and communion with the Bishop and the entire Church." DMLP, no. 39. See also CIC, c. 278.

61   "One cannot sufficiently recommend to priests a life lived in common and directed entirely toward their sacred ministry; the practice of having frequent meetings with a fraternal exchange of ideas, counsel and experience with their brother priests; the movement to form associations which encourage priestly holiness." St. Paul VI, *Sacerdotalis Caelibatus (On the Celibacy of the Priest)*, June 24, 1967, no. 80. "Some practice of common life is highly recommended to clerics; where it exists, it must be preserved as far as possible." CIC, c. 280.

62   "The experience of this common life has been rather positive in many places because it has represented a real form of support for priests: created is a family environment, with the permission of the local Ordinary it is possible to have a chapel for the Blessed Sacrament, and it is also possible to pray together, etc. . . . Many are the cases of priests who have found an important source of help for both their personal needs and the exercise of their pastoral ministry in the adoption of opportune forms of communitarian life." DMLP, no. 39.

region can at least coordinate the same day of rest each week and so more easily arrange for priestly gatherings, prayer, and recreation.

81 Whatever the format, priestly fraternity can play an important role in our ongoing formation. Our fraternity is a matter not of instrumentalizing friendship for the sake of our personal development, but rather of highlighting ways that our friendships already are, or could be, a source of mutual growth. It is hoped that the specific suggestions in this document regarding the fraternal means of ongoing formation will promote and expand the fraternity that is one of the great blessings of our priesthood.

EPISCOPAL MEANS

82 Among the chief duties of a diocesan bishop is to care for his priests. He sees to it, for example, that they have a livable income and proper medical care. He ensures that their rectories are decent. He observes their anniversaries and visits them in the hospital when they are ill. He celebrates their funerals and commends them to God when they have died. A diocesan bishop's care for his priests, though, goes beyond this. He wants for them what he wants for himself, that is, to thrive, to grow in all dimensions of formation, and to strive always to become a more authentic Christian, a better man, and a holier priest.[63]

83 Episcopal means of formation are found in the person of the diocesan bishop himself, as when he directly encourages priests to embrace ongoing formation and sets an example for them. He makes priests' gatherings, retreats, and formation events a priority and, whenever possible, is "present in person and taking part in an interested and

---

63 "The Bishop's responsibility is based on the fact that priests receive their priesthood from him and share his pastoral solicitude for the People of God. He is responsible for ongoing formation, the purpose of which is to ensure that all his priests are generously faithful to the gift and ministry received, that they are priests such as the People of God wishes to have and has a 'right' to." PDV, no. 79. See also CIC, c. 384; Congregation for Bishops, *Apostolorum Successores (Directory for the Pastoral Ministry of Bishops),* February 22, 2004, nos. 75-83.

friendly way."[64] Episcopal means also include diocesan efforts such as priest convocations, retreats, days of recollection, and study days, as well as mentoring programs and many other ways that dioceses can support priests who wish to continue their formation.[65]

84 Newly ordained priests require particular care as their priestly identity matures. They are encountering their first major challenges, and their initial enthusiasm is being tested. Without supervision and assistance, newly ordained priests can sometimes feel isolated and adrift. With the concern, availability, and ready assistance of the diocesan bishop, however, those first years can be a wonderful opportunity to grow and to chart a course in their priestly lives that will serve them, and the people they serve, for years to come.[66]

Aids to Personal, Fraternal, and Episcopal Means

85 Apart from the three main sources of ongoing formation—personal, fraternal, and episcopal—regional and national organizations as well as countless grassroots efforts provide ongoing formation to priests. The opportunities afforded by the Internet, including digital platforms and virtual learning, have vastly expanded the reach of these efforts. In fact, the greater struggle today lies not in finding opportunities to grow, but rather in selecting well among the options

---

64   PDV, no. 79.
65   "It is desirable that this formation be promoted in each Diocese by a priest or group of priests, specifically prepared for it and officially appointed to assist in ongoing formation." *Ratio Fundamentalis*, no. 82. "Obviously this must not make the Bishop and the entire presbyterate forget their grave responsibility in avoiding any loneliness caused by negligence with respect to priestly communion. It is incumbent upon the Diocese to decide how to hold encounters among priests so they may experience being together, learning from one another and being of assistance to one another, because no one is a priest all on his own, and exclusively in this communion with the Bishop may each priest render his service." DMLP, no. 115.
66   "A positive experience in many places has also been the organization, under the guidance of the Bishop, of brief encounters during the year for young priests, for example, those with less than ten years of priesthood, in order to be closer by their side while accompanying them during these early years; they will undoubtedly be occasions as well to discuss the priestly spirituality, challenges for ministers, and pastoral praxis, etc., in settings of fraternal and priestly togetherness." DMLP, no. 111.

available. Moreover, however useful the online options might be, they can never entirely replace live interaction with other priests.

86 At their best, however, these adjunct means of formation can be a great blessing to a priest who is serious about his continued formation. They can supplement the personal, fraternal, and episcopal means of formation and provide enrichment and support particularly for priests who lack structured support in their region or diocese.

ONGOING FORMATION AT DIFFERENT STAGES OF LIFE

87 We read in the Scriptures that James and John, the sons of Zebedee, came to Jesus one day and asked him for a favor. They wanted to sit on his right and on his left in glory. Jesus asked them, "Can you drink the cup that I drink or be baptized with the baptism with which I am baptized?" They replied with youthful earnestness, "We can!" (Mk 10:38-39). They could not know what they were promising. They did not know what life had in store for them, the suffering they would have to endure. Perhaps that was for the best, because their hearts might have failed them. What they did know is that Jesus would be with them through it all.

88 On the day of our ordination, we too were ready for anything. We gave our earnest *We can!* like James and John did. And though we did not know what life would bring or what suffering we would encounter, we did know that Jesus would be with us, whatever lay ahead. There have been changes along the way: in our ministry, in our relationships, in our health, and in many other circumstances of life. For an approach to ongoing formation to be effective, it must recognize these changes and accommodate them. What follows are sketches of typical phases of life experienced by many priests, as well

as some ways that ongoing formation might be customized to suit their particular needs.

EARLY PRIESTHOOD

89   For the first years after ordination, the lessons of seminary need to be assimilated in a new way and applied to the actual experience of priestly life and ministry. The gentle and patient hand of a mentor, as well as a wise spiritual director, is vitally important. With the shift away from a structured seminary life, a young priest will want to have a suitable plan of life that is both challenging and realistic. He will need regular periods of rest, prayer, and retreat, when he can step aside from the activity of ministry so he can process his new life in a supernatural light. The intellectual and pastoral formation of a younger priest should include a review of the canons and liturgical texts pertaining to the administration of the sacraments and parish life, as well as faculties, norms, and policies issued by the diocesan bishop. These reviews can benefit the intellectual and pastoral formation of a younger priest, especially when he considers practical questions arising from his ministerial experience.[67]

90   A new priest enters into many new and enriching relationships after he leaves seminary. He is assigned to a parish, where he meets new people and begins to develop relationships with staff, many of whom are women, and with families and other parishioners. His interactions with his own family and previous friends need to adjust to his new responsibilities. Relationships with other priests, including friends from seminary, must now compete with the many demands on his time and attention. Navigating all these relationships is not easy. The

---

67   "During the early years of priesthood it is necessary to organize annual formation encounters for dealing in greater depth with appropriate theological, juridical, spiritual and cultural themes, as well as special sessions dedicated to moral, pastoral and liturgical questions, etc. Such encounters may also be occasions to renew the faculty of confession as stipulated by the *Code of Canon Law* and by the Bishop." DMLP, no. 111.

steady guidance of more experienced priests can help the new priest to do so.

91   Careful selection of the pastor of a newly ordained priest is essential because "the first destination should respond above all to the need to set young priests on the right path."[68] In his priestly example and friendship, concern for his younger brother, and capacity to offer gentle suggestions and corrections, such a pastor will have a profound impact on the trajectory of a man's entire priesthood. In many respects our first pastor is the first teacher in our priestly lives and one whose influence is most enduring.[69] Many young priests are also eager to have a more personal relationship with their diocesan bishop. A diocesan bishop's accessibility to his newly ordained priests in their joys and struggles—and his solicitude for their welfare, both personally and through his vicar for clergy—will yield tremendous benefits throughout their lives.[70]

92   Diocesan bishops and those responsible for ongoing formation therefore need to pay particular attention to the growth of their newly ordained priests. No less importantly, those young priests must take seriously their own responsibility to seek the means of formation they most need during the exciting but also demanding first years of priestly ministry. "These first years," the DMLP states, "constitute a necessary verification of their initial formation after the first delicate impact with reality, and are the most decisive ones for the future.

---

68   DMLP, no. 100.

69   "It is desirable that accompaniment by confreres of exemplary life and pastoral zeal be promoted, so that they can help young priests to experience a cordial and active participation in the life of the entire diocesan presbyterate. . . . It is good to set up a system of personal accompaniment of young priests, to promote and maintain the quality of their ministry, so that they can embrace their first pastoral challenges with enthusiasm. It is the Pastor *[parochus]* above all who should assume responsibility for this, or whichever priest it is to whom the young priest has first been sent." *Ratio Fundamentalis*, no. 83.

70   "Moreover, it would seem useful to underscore the need especially for young priests to be introduced to an authentic journey of faith in the presbyterate or in the parish community, accompanied by the Bishop and by the brother priests assigned to that task." DMLP, no. 111.

Young priests therefore require harmonious maturation in order to be able to cope with moments of difficulty with faith and fortitude."[71]

TRANSITIONS

93 After surmounting the challenges that attend the first years of priesthood, a man starts to encounter transitions that again require particular attention. Leaving his first parish is often a painful experience. The commitment to celibacy can seem especially keen to a young priest who must uproot himself from the parishioners and families he has grown to love and serve. When he reports to his new assignment, the loneliness can be a bit overwhelming. Personal and fraternal means of support will be especially important in those moments.

94 In the early and middle years of priesthood, relationships with brother priests often undergo changes. Priests usually need to scale down some seminary friendships to focus time and energy on a more manageable number. New priest friendships also start to take root. These too are important transitions that call for suitable preparation and support.

95 Many priests today assume the responsibilities of a pastor only a few years after ordination. While they strive to be good shepherds to the people they serve, they will need to learn new leadership skills, church management, and financial accountability, as well as making key contacts within the diocesan curia. Of particular importance will be seasoned pastor-mentors who can guide new pastors well. It is not enough that these mentors be good pastors; they must be able to instill the qualities of good pastors in others. They will likely also be the best pastors to guide and form parochial vicars.

---

71   DMLP, no. 111.

96 Other positions that priests might assume include hospital or campus chaplains, vocation directors, seminary faculty, or chancery positions. These men undergo the usual challenges of a change in life while also needing particular formation for their new positions.

97 Finally, transitions include the ordinary, but still difficult, changes that occur in every human life. When priests experience the death of their parents, for example, they are especially prone to difficulties. Priests undergoing these pivotal moments in life need extra support and guidance from friends and mentors.

Middle Years of Priesthood

98 As they enter middle age, men sometimes experience a "midlife crisis" that tempts them to reconsider the direction their life is taking and the commitments that they have made. Married men, for instance, can be tempted to question their previous choices about their spouse, family, or career. A priest, like other men, is called to respond to these temptations with fortitude, supernatural outlook, and joyful perseverance. They are an opportunity for him to rededicate himself to the Lord, to his priesthood, and to the Church.[72] Nevertheless, midlife is not a period of life to be ignored; the support of others, including the advice of older priests, will help priests at this age to emerge from the crisis more confident and peaceful than ever.

99 In middle age, men must also begin to pay more attention to their physical health. Without becoming fastidious, priests need to make reasonable efforts to remain fit and healthy through good nutrition, exercise, wholesome habits, and sufficient sleep. Healthy aging begins

---

72 "They [that is, middle-aged priests] need encouragement, intelligent appreciation and enhancement, and a new deepening of formation in all its dimensions in order to rethink themselves and what they do; to reawaken the motivations underlying the sacred ministry; to do serious thinking about pastoral methods in the light of what is essential, communion among priests of the presbyterate, and friendship with the Bishop; to surmount any sense of exhaustion, frustration and solitude; to rediscover the wellsprings of the priestly spirituality." DMLP, no. 112.

in these years; efforts should include regular physicals and proper medical care. Ongoing formation helps priests anticipate, manage, and gracefully cope with these natural changes.

Senior and "Retired" Clergy

100 A stage of life that is sometimes overlooked in discussions of ongoing formation is that of senior clergy. The transition into an older age group, often away from formal administrative duties, is a life change as serious as any other.

101 Some senior priests continue to live in a rectory or other forms of common priestly life; others choose to live on their own. Many priests eventually need to move into an assisted living facility. Priests, however, do not retire, even when required to resign their office due to age.[73] Their new status simply means a change in their pastoral ministry. In their daily Mass and prayer, for which they have perhaps more opportunity and leisure, senior priests can do immeasurable good for the Church at large and for their fellow priests still in the field. They have an opportunity "to deepen the contemplative sense of the priestly life, rediscover and savor the doctrinal treasures of what they have already studied, and feel they are useful, as they rightly are, insofar as being of utmost value in suitable forms of true and proper ministry, especially as expert confessors and spiritual directors."[74] Senior priests with flexibility in their schedules provide valuable service to local, regional, or even national Catholic organizations. Their experience and wisdom are a treasure of profound worth to their younger brothers, and every diocese would do well to tap into that source of spiritual wealth.[75]

---

73 See CIC, c. 538 §3.
74 DMLP, no. 113.
75 "In particular, they [senior priests] will be able to share with others their own experiences, provide encouragement, receptiveness, listening and serenity to their confreres, and be available if they are summoned 'to become effective teachers and trainers of other priests' (PDV, no. 77)." DMLP, no. 113.

102 Senior priests can also be of great help offering Mass coverage for short periods of time, so that other priests can go on retreat, spend time with brother priests, care for family members, or engage in their own ongoing formation. In these and many other ways, senior clergy can be a tremendous source of vitality for an entire presbyterate, if they are prepared to assume their new role through proper support and adequate care.

103 These, then, are some of the means of formation that we will address in greater detail in the chapters that follow—and some of the stages of life for which a plan of ongoing formation should be adapted. We hope that the specific recommendations in each dimension of formation will provide enough detail to suggest concrete means for growth, yet allow for their application to each priest's particular needs and circumstances. After all, we do not know exactly what Jesus did with his Apostles during those forty days of companionship and formation after his Resurrection, but we can be sure that each one received what he needed to keep growing. The rest of this document seeks to provide the same.

CHAPTER THREE
Human Formation

104 The four dimensions of priestly formation—human, spiritual, intellectual, and pastoral—are distinct but closely interconnected. They can be compared to the elements of the Lord's Cross. The spiritual dimension, represented by the vertical bar of the Cross, unites us to God. The intellectual dimension, represented by the horizontal bar, takes us into the mind of Christ. The pastoral dimension, represented by the Body of the Lord, forms us to serve Jesus in our neighbor. And the human dimension, according to this image, is the soil in which the Cross is planted. That soil is the subject of this chapter.

105 As ordained men, we commonly understand that grace perfects and presupposes nature, and the grace of the priesthood is no exception.[76] The better the soil in which that grace is planted, the more abundant the yield. However, our humanity is not merely the setting in which our priesthood grows. It is also a reflection of the humanity shared by Jesus, our High Priest. The Letter to the Hebrews teaches that "we do not have a high priest who is unable to sympathize with our weaknesses, but one who has similarly been tested in every way, yet without sin" (4:15). In developing our human nature to its fullest, then, we are also conforming ourselves more closely to the perfect humanity of the Lord.[77]

---

76   See St. Thomas Aquinas, *Summa Theologicae*, I, q. 1, art. 8 ad 2.
77   "The priest, who is called to be a 'living image' of Jesus Christ, head and shepherd of the Church, should seek to reflect in himself, as far as possible, the human perfection which shines forth in the incarnate Son of God and which is reflected with particular liveliness in his attitudes toward others as we see narrated in the Gospels." PDV, no. 43.

106 This chapter identifies some markers for the human dimension of the priesthood and then proposes various personal, fraternal, and ecclesial means to reach those markers.

MARKERS OF THE HUMAN DIMENSION
HUMAN MATURITY

107 Maturity, meaning completeness or full development, is the overarching goal of all human formation. "Human maturity" refers to a life approaching a certain fullness, characterized by habits that lead to human flourishing and continued growth. A well-formed conscience directs the mature individual to his authentic good; a will strengthened by grace and good habits is capable of pursuing that good.[78] Psychological and emotional obstacles that hinder virtue are recognized and addressed. A mature person is steadfast and able to weather the storms of life, humbly seeking help when needed.

108 A crucial aspect of maturity is affective, or emotional, maturity.[79] An affectively mature person enjoys harmony between intellect and passions. Emotions are not ignored or repressed. Neither are they given free rein. Rather, they are acknowledged and considered. They are integrated into a larger identity that can judge the suitability of particular emotions at particular times and respond accordingly. The passions, in other words, are under the authority of reason, which harnesses their power and directs them toward our true good.

109 Understanding the importance of maturity in a priest is not difficult. Pastoral work demands the stability of mind and heart that distinguishes a mature individual. Moreover, he needs enough

---

78 "This [due human maturity] will be chiefly attested by a certain stability of character, the ability to make carefully weighed decisions, and a sound judgment of events and people." OT, no. 11.

79 "Human maturation: albeit difficult to specify in contents, this undoubtedly implies equilibrium and harmony in the integration of propensities and values, psychological and affective stability, prudence, objectivity in judgment, fortitude in self-control, sociability, etc." DMLP, no. 93.

resiliency to handle his own struggles while sharing, to some extent, the struggles of others. When a priest works with souls, many disclose strong feelings such as anger, sadness, and fear. If the priest has not handled those feelings well himself, he will find it challenging to help others do so.

110 In addition, affective maturity is an indispensable ingredient in living celibacy appropriately. Such maturity represents a command of self that makes possible the self-gift of celibacy: "able to renounce anything that is a threat to it, vigilant over both body and spirit, and capable of esteem and respect in interpersonal relationships between men and women."[80] In addition, "the priest is then able to encourage and nurture the 'feminine genius' which women offer to the Church and the world."[81] This also benefits the priest himself as he experiences this complementarity. Affective maturity in a celibate priest means that his capacity to love is directed to its authentic good in his life and ministry. It means that he can donate himself fully and joyfully for the people he serves.

UNITY OF LIFE

111 A priest who lives a unity of life is not fragmented or compartmentalized. He has integrated the various dimensions of formation into a life of virtue.[82] His interior life, for instance, does not make him aloof or eccentric. His pastoral generosity does not make him neglect important friendships. His human interests do not cause him to become worldly. The priest who lives a unified life does not posture for different audiences. He has one personality, refracted

---

80   PDV, no. 44.
81   *Mulieris Dignitatem,* no. 31.
82   "It is important for the priest, who is called to accompany others through the journey of life up to the threshold of death, to have the right balance of heart and mind, reason and feeling, body and soul, and to be humanly integrated." Benedict XVI, Letter to Seminarians, October 18, 2010, no. 6.

into different circumstances and relationships, but always emerging from the same source.[83]

112 The common thread that ties together the various components of the personality of the priest is his relationship with Jesus, who calls him to participate in his pastoral charity.[84] He approaches all of his activities and interests in a spirit of Christ's pastoral charity.[85] At the heart of his plan of life is daily prayer, which encounters Jesus as the source of priestly life. Surrounding those key spiritual exercises is a balanced life of work, recreation, exercise, diet, and vacation.[86] The priest has a healthy love for the world and fosters an interest in culture, beauty, and nature without falling into the superficiality of secularism.

113 In addition, unity of life includes the way a priest approaches the various moments and situations of his life. It means that the priest is always the same person in all his dealings with others, whether those occur in person or through digital communication. Unity of life excludes any sense of a double life, obscuring of one's identity, or any other behavior that conflicts with being a priest. This unity of life is not just about avoiding duplicity and scandal. The priest is a public person, which means that he accepts the need for a great deal

---

83   "Of special importance is the capacity to relate to others. This is truly fundamental for a person who is called to be responsible for a community and to be a 'man of communion.'" PDV, no. 43.

84   "Priests attain to the unity of their lives by uniting themselves with Christ in acknowledging the Father's will and in the gift of themselves on behalf of the flock committed to them. Thus, by assuming the role of the Good Shepherd, they will find in the very exercise of pastoral love the bond of priestly perfection which will unify their lives and activities." Second Vatican Council, *Presbyterorum Ordinis (Decree on the Ministry and Life of Priests)*, no. 14, in *The Documents of Vatican II*, ed. Walter M. Abbott (New York: Corpus Books, 1966). Subsequently cited as PO.

85   "This same pastoral charity is the dynamic inner principle capable of unifying the many different activities of the priest. In virtue of this pastoral charity the essential and permanent demand for unity between the priest's interior life and all his external actions and the obligations of the ministry can be properly fulfilled, a demand particularly urgent in a socio - cultural and ecclesial context strongly marked by complexity, fragmentation and dispersion. Only by directing every moment and every one of his acts toward the fundamental choice to "give his life for the flock" can the priest guarantee this unity which is vital and indispensable for his harmony and spiritual balance." PDV, no. 23.

86   See CIC, c. 283, §2.

of transparency in his life. It also involves knowing and embracing at all times who one is and intentionally living in accord with one's identity both alone and with others. The priest's unity of life springs from gratitude at being personally called by Jesus; it is an overflow of that joy into the decisions and interactions of his life. A priest with unity of life knows he shares the pastoral charity of Christ and always seeks to care for souls. Of course, he prudently considers the circumstances of his interaction and may not always speak explicitly about the faith—but in all his encounters, the priest who possesses unity of life seeks to treat others with a refined kindness that reflects the charity of Jesus.

CAPACITY FOR FATHERHOOD

114 The priest's spiritual fatherhood is more than a mere metaphor for his ministry. Like a natural father, he shares in the Fatherhood of God by generating life and loving in a distinctly paternal way.[87] For example, the priest provides for his people in the order of grace, particularly by administering the sacraments. He guides them along the way of truth and salvation, especially in his preaching and teaching. He protects them from harmful spiritual and moral influences through his courageous and loving counsel and personal sacrifice. These and other paternal responsibilities depend upon a constellation of human virtues that natural and spiritual fathers have in common. They are important markers of human formation, as the following examples outline:

---

87 "Through the gift of celibacy the priest also acquires that spiritual yet real fatherhood which is universal in dimension and assumes concrete expression particularly towards the community entrusted to him." DMLP, no. 80.

a. Good fathers exhibit the *capacity to sacrifice*, to be generous. Can a priest spend himself for others, or does he live primarily for himself?[88]

b. *Discipline and responsibility* are needed in a father. Is a priest reliable, can he keep a schedule, and does he show up on time, dedicating himself to the task at hand?

c. A father particularly needs *humility* in the exercise of paternal authority. Jesus told his Apostles that among the Gentiles, "the great ones make their authority . . . felt," while the one who "wishes to be great among you shall be your servant" (Mt 20:25-26). Like all Christian fathers, the priest wants to use his authority forbearingly so that it truly fosters the growth of those entrusted to his care. A father needs to rejoice with those who rejoice and to weep with those who weep.[89] His sympathy with the people he serves often opens him to a very deep encounter.

d. *Sincerity* is an important virtue in a father. Is the priest a man of his word, open and authentic, and transparent with his spiritual director, with his friends, with God himself?

e. Good fathers are *patient and kind*. Is a priest gentle with the souls entrusted to his care? Can he be both tender and strong like the best fathers? As a spiritual father, is he a man of encouragement who knows how to lift up and sympathetically exhort his people to a higher way of life?[90]

---

88   "The ministry of the priest is therefore also the ministry of fatherhood. Through his dedication to souls many are those generated to the new life in Christ. This is a true spiritual fatherhood as St. Paul exclaimed: 'You might have thousands of guardians in Christ, but not more than one father and it was I who begot you in Christ Jesus by preaching the Good News' (1 Cor 4:15)." DMLP, no. 24.

89   See Rm 12:15.

90   "Revealing himself at all times as priest, he will therefore exercise his spiritual mission with kindness and firmness, humility and a spirit of service, opening himself to compassion, participating in the sufferings inflicted upon men by the various forms of poverty, spiritual and material, old and new. He will also know how to bend over with mercy upon the difficult and uncertain journey of the conversion of sinners, to whom he will reserve the gift of truth and the patient, encouraging benevolence of the Good Shepherd, who does not reprove the lost sheep, but loads it onto his shoulders and celebrates its return to the fold (cf. Lk 15:4-7)." DMLP, no. 41.

f. A father needs *courage* to protect his family. The priest must be a good shepherd, not a mercenary who runs at the first sign of a wolf. Can a priest take a stand? Will he be loyal to Christ and to the Gospel? Is he able to teach the truth even when it is hard for his people to hear? Is he willing to be rejected or sidelined for it?

g. Finally, a good father is *committed*. Is a priest able to persevere in his vocation? Can he weather difficult times? Is he committed to becoming a better priest?

HEALTHY CHASTITY

115 A crucial marker in the human formation of a priest is his capacity to live healthy chastity. Chastity is fundamentally a positive trait, because through it a man gains the self-mastery to love in a sexually mature way. Chastity is "the successful integration of sexuality within the person and thus the inner unity of man in his bodily and spiritual being."[91] Though the priest is celibate, he is still a sexual being; chastity ensures that his masculine love is well directed.[92]

116 Such a view of chastity presumes that the body is good. The human body enables us to interact, communicate, and love. If God did not want us to love him and others as sexual beings, he would have made us angels. Nevertheless, in Original Sin our passions, and especially our sexual urges, became unmoored from the dominion of reason. It is the virtue of chastity which tempers and channels the powerful sexual drive in a wholesome way. Chastity is not the most important

---

91   CCC, no. 2337.

92   "It cannot be forgotten that celibacy is vivified by the practice of the virtue of chastity, which can be lived only through the cultivation of purity with supernatural and human maturity insofar as essential for the development of the talent of the vocation. It is not possible to love Christ and others with an impure heart. The virtue of purity makes it possible to live what the Apostle said: 'Therefore, glorify God in your body!' (1 Cor 6:20). Then again, when this virtue is lacking, all the other dimensions are damaged." DMLP, no. 82.

virtue, although it is an indispensable condition for holiness. We cannot make progress in the spiritual life without it.[93]

117 Chastity is a training in freedom: both freedom to have authentic communion with others and freedom from the shackles of sin. The "alternative is clear: either man governs his passions and finds peace, or he lets himself be dominated by them and becomes unhappy."[94] Chastity is like the ribcage that protects the heart. The ribs are sturdy and unbending, like the demands of chastity—but they are there to guard something precious. Chastity, then, is a way of glorifying God and showing gratitude for his love, as St. Paul wrote to the Corinthians: "Avoid immorality. Every other sin a person commits is outside the body, but the immoral person sins against his own body. Do you not know that your body is a temple of the Holy Spirit within you, whom you have from God, and that you are not your own? For you have been purchased at a price. Therefore glorify God in your body" (1 Cor 6:18-20).

118 Chastity is particularly important for a man called to live apostolic celibacy. Such a life means more than simply renouncing sexual relations; it has a supernatural purpose.[95] Jesus called men to live celibacy "for the sake of the kingdom of heaven" (Mt 19:12). It is a way of loving that opens a man's heart to all and is a privileged way of living spiritual fatherhood. Celibacy has a unique capacity to foster an undivided heart for the affairs of the Lord and the good

---

93   "Whoever wants to remain faithful to his baptismal promises and resist temptations will want to adopt the *means* for doing so: self-knowledge, practice of an ascesis adapted to the situations that confront him, obedience to God's commandments, exercise of the moral virtues, and fidelity to prayer. 'Indeed it is through chastity that we are gathered together and led back to the unity from which we were fragmented into multiplicity' (St. Augustine, *Conf.* 10, 29, 40: PL 32, 796)." CCC, no. 2340.
94   CCC, no. 2339.
95   "Celibacy is a gift received from divine mercy as the choice freely and gratefully accepting a particular vocation of love for God and others. It must not be understood and lived as if it were no more than a collateral effect of the priesthood." DMLP, no. 81.

of his people (see 1 Cor 7:32-33).[96] It is an imitation of Jesus' own celibate love for the Church, as Pope St. John Paul II observed. "The Church, as the spouse of Jesus Christ," he wrote, "wishes to be loved by the priest in the total and exclusive manner in which Jesus Christ her head and spouse loved her."[97]

119 Because a celibate priest's heart and body are reserved for God and his Church alone, the self-mastery of chastity is essential. The priest's vocation is incompatible with any deliberate genital activity, alone or with another person. Any use of pornography or masturbation, for instance, is a grave sin (as it is for anyone else) and also a violation of his celibate promise. God in his mercy will heal and restore anyone who goes to him with a contrite heart, of course, but he also promises grace and help to a man who wishes to be free of these sins.[98] We cannot, and need not, settle for mediocrity in this area. Living our celibate commitment well is not only a key marker of human formation but a profound witness to a world steeped in the misery of sexual sin.

120 Chastity is the virtue that enables men and women to love well, regardless of their vocation. "The chaste person maintains the integrity of the powers of life and love placed in him. This integrity ensures the unity of the person; it is opposed to any behavior that would impair it."[99] Everyone is called to give life to others, in the natural or supernatural order; and chastity strengthens and protects that capacity to love. This is no less true in the life of the priest, for whom chastity plays a vital role by directing his heart to the genuine good of those he serves.

---

96   See CIC, c. 277 §1.
97   PDV, no. 29.
98   "While it is true that today's world poses various difficulties regarding the living of holy purity, it is all the truer that the Lord abundantly showers his grace and offers the practical means for practicing this virtue with joy and happiness." DMLP, no. 82.
99   CCC, no. 2338.

Capacity for Friendship

121 Celibacy does not exclude affection and friendship. In fact, a key marker of any healthy human life is the capacity to make and keep properly ordered friendships, one of the great goods of life. Jesus himself showed us the importance of friendship in his love for friends such as Lazarus, Martha, and Mary, as well as his Apostles. He spoke from his heart to his friends on the night before he died: "I have called you friends, because I have told you everything I have heard from my Father" (Jn 15:15).

122 Friendship is a good in itself, being a form of human communion and an example of neighborly love that Jesus identified as a key feature of a Christian life. Friendships are also a school of charity, a source of consolation in difficult times, and a stimulus to courage when friends tackle challenges together.[100] Priests desire solid friendships to help them live their vocation well and trust God in every encounter.

123 One's first relationships in life are with parents, siblings, extended family, and childhood friends. Some of these friendships will hopefully continue to nourish a priest throughout his life. Many priests make friendships in adulthood with both men and women, and these relationships often continue to grow and mature after ordination. Such friends can frequently provide a helpful perspective that is less constrained by ecclesiastical assumptions.

124 Friendships with the people he serves, given proper boundaries, can also be a healthy source of joy and genuine growth for the priest. [101]Pastoral charity dictates that the priest give himself for the sake of

---

100 "Friendship is one of life's gifts and a grace from God. Through our friends, the Lord refines us and leads us to maturity. Faithful friends, who stand at our side in times of difficulty, are also a reflection of the Lord's love, his gentle and consoling presence in our lives." Francis, *Christus Vivit (Christ Is Alive)*, March 25, 2019, no. 151.

101 See CIC, c. 277 §2.

his people without seeking for himself.[102] The people are not given to him for his sake. Yet, in his giving of himself for them, he comes into a genuine friendship with his people, which naturally helps the priest grow as a man. A healthy priest will have respectful friendship with his people and allow them to form him into a better man and minister.

125 Above all, friendship with brother priests enjoys a unique place in our lives. The Second Vatican Council taught that each priest is united in special bonds of apostolic charity, ministry, and brotherhood with the other members of this priesthood. This bond has been manifested from ancient times in the liturgy, when the priests present at an ordination are invited to impose hands together with the ordaining bishop on the new candidate and, with united hearts, to concelebrate the Eucharist. Each and every priest, therefore, is united with his fellow priests in a bond of charity, prayer, and total cooperation. In this manner, they manifest that unity which Christ willed, namely, that his own be perfected in one so that the world might know that the Son was sent by the Father.[103]

126 All priests, especially those united in a common presbyterate, should endeavor to be friends. Priests who strive to find common ground with diocesan brothers despite differences in age, experiences, or viewpoints seldom regret the effort. In addition to these broader friendships, most priests also have a handful of closer friends with whom they can share their joys and struggles. The best friendships are typically the result of a conscious choice on the part of both individuals to make it work. Some priests by temperament will be better at this than others, but all can learn. This effort means intentionally finding common interests, being open to deeper

---

102　"The gift of self has no limits, marked as it is by the same apostolic and missionary zeal of Christ, the good shepherd, who said: 'And I have other sheep, that are not of this fold; I must bring them also, and they will heed my voice. So there shall be one flock, one shepherd' (Jn 10:16)." PDV, no. 23.

103　See PO, no. 8.

conversations, and above all, jealously guarding the time to make and sustain friendships. Aristotle said that it takes fifteen pounds of salt to make a good friend[104]—meaning that friends must enjoy enough meals together to consume that much salt.

127 The goal is to foster the conditions in which genuine friendships can flourish: friendships that are deep and sincere, where we can truly be ourselves, where we are accepted as we are. Friendships like these, free of unhealthy dependencies and exclusivity, are the priest's greatest source of strength apart from his relationship with the Lord. They are undoubtedly a marker of a thriving human life.

TEMPERANCE

128 Denying the excessive cravings of human nature is a final marker of human formation in the priest. Temperance applies, first and foremost, to the use of food, drink, and tobacco products, but it can involve other things that we can inordinately use and desire. Because we are never free of the effects of Original Sin, God gives us the capacity for the virtue of temperance, which we cultivate by his grace to help us deal with concupiscence and gain greater freedom in our life.[105] Apart from its benefit for human thriving, temperance is a way of mortifying the flesh and offers an important witness to our self-indulgent culture. It is a sign of credibility in preaching the Gospel. In addition, many people around the world do not have enough food even to be temperate; those of us who live in prosperous nations can at least strive to be closer to the poor by moderating our meals.

---

104   In *Eudemian Ethics*, 1238a1, Aristotle said literally a "peck" of salt, which is a quarter-bushel, or roughly fifteen pounds.

105   "It [original sin] is a deprivation of original holiness and justice, but human nature has not been totally corrupted: it is wounded in the natural powers proper to it; subject to ignorance, suffering, and the dominion of death; and inclined to sin—an inclination to evil that is called 'concupiscence.' Baptism, by imparting the life of Christ's grace, erases original sin and turns a man back toward God, but the consequences for nature, weakened and inclined to evil, persist in man and summon him to spiritual battle (cf. Council of Trent: DS 1513)." CCC, no. 405.

129 Restraining alcohol and tobacco consumption, too, has both a personal and an apostolic benefit. The number of priests in the grip of substance dependency is not negligible. Curbing the desire for nicotine and alcohol will lead to longer, more active, and happier lives. It will also ensure that substance abuse does not become an obstacle to a priest's ministry, as it has, sadly, in too many cases. Often living alone, sometimes in isolation from brother priests and other friends, a priest is particularly susceptible to the excessive use of alcohol and nicotine and must make concrete resolutions to keep its use in healthy bounds.

130 Another area for temperance is the proper use of digital media and personal devices. Apart from the need to avoid offensive and inappropriate content, temperance means that these technologies do not become a form of bondage for the priest. Many people today, even those who have embraced digital media for good purposes, find themselves attached to digital media and devices that cultivate compulsive behavior. The priest, like everyone else who uses these tools, must offset these pressures with equally deliberate choices. He might, for instance, limit his daily usage of certain content sources, install accountability software, refrain from carrying his digital device on him at the rectory, or make his living space a digital-free zone. In addition, a temperate priest considers regulating which websites and news sources he engages with, particularly those that are irresponsible, inflammatory, or disingenuous.[106] Temperance is a way of humbly acknowledging that concupiscence is real, that we are weaker than we might imagine, and that we are susceptible to bad influences. Excessive technology use can be a distraction that consumes time, energy, and attention. It can become an impediment

---

106 Priests should be aware that online activity—email, browsing, texting, social media, and so on—is never absolutely private. The prudence and integrity the priest exercises in using such media are for the sake of not only his own soul, but also the reputation of the priesthood and the Church as well as the good of the faithful.

to silence and recollection. Moderating our intake of digital devices and content is one way to express that humility.[107]

131 A final way to practice temperance pertains to the craving for material goods. The priest promises to live a simple life, a pledge that he should express in concrete ways.[108] As in the other forms of temperance such as food, drink, and social media, the priest's simplicity of life is a visible witness to gospel values, especially in the highly consumeristic and materialistic culture of the United States today. We do not deny the goodness of Creation and of material goods in themselves, but a simple lifestyle preaches more with actions than with words. A diocesan priest has a unique opportunity to give this witness. He is challenged to live in the world, shoulder to shoulder with his parishioners, without caving in to the wider culture's relentless pressure to indulge the appetite for more or better possessions.

132 Simplicity of life cannot remain simply a compelling idea; it expresses itself concretely in the priest's choice of car, for instance, and of phone, computer, dining habits, vacations, and hobbies.[109] The priest who lives simply gives a personal witness of good stewardship by tithing his income and giving generously to the parish and other personal charities. He makes larger purchases carefully, consulting others when needed, and gets quality things that he takes care of so they will last. He manages his personal finances prudently but without spending an inordinate amount of time on them. He plans carefully for the expenses that often emerge later in life, such as medical bills, so that his diocese is not overly burdened financially. Above all, his simplicity of life is ordered not only to external poverty but, even more importantly, to

---

107   See CIC, c. 666.
108   See CIC, c. 282 §1.
109   See CIC, c. 285 §§1-2.

internal poverty. A priest's surroundings and possessions may be ever so simple—but if he is not internally detached from his goods, then he is not yet living the virtue of temperance.

MEANS OF HUMAN FORMATION

PERSONAL MEANS

133 Many of the personal means of human formation are immediately obvious from the markers identified above. Virtues of fatherhood like responsibility, patience, humility, and courage all call for continual effort, correspondence to grace, and concrete resolutions to grow. There are no shortcuts to growing in virtue. Forging friendships, too, requires a personal investment of time and initiative. Building habits of temperance demands self-denial and daily mortification in the use of food, drink, the Internet, and possessions.

134 Given its importance, the priest should pursue the virtue of chastity with particular determination. Many circumstances can aggravate the fight for holy purity. Excessive trust of self, lack of prayer, failing to appreciate one's vulnerabilities, loneliness, love of comfort, discouragement in the face of temptations, and inadequate boundaries in friendships, among others, can present obstacles.[110] Identifying and surmounting these obstacles, often in spiritual direction, makes the priest's progress in holy purity much easier.

135 The means of ongoing growth in chastity are no different from what priests first learned in the seminary, and they include both natural and supernatural means. Natural means include guarding the senses, imagination, and memory; developing good friendships; cultivating an ordered and balanced life; and regularly exposing oneself to beauty in nature and art. Supernatural means include regular prayer and

---

110   See CIC, c. 277 §2.

confession, daily mortifications, sincerity with close priest friends and with a spiritual director, and filial devotion to Our Lady and St. Joseph. Continued progress in chastity is a lifelong endeavor, but countless celibate priests have lived their vocation with integrity and peace and have demonstrated that it can be a joyful, healthy way of life.

136 More generally, candid self-awareness and sincerity with a spiritual director or trusted friend will help identify where the priest needs other growth, especially in the markers of human maturity. Fears, blind spots, and bad habits can hamper his free exercise of the will, and such limitations are important topics of examination for personal prayer and spiritual direction. Gaps in maturity, especially affective maturity, need to be addressed methodically and energetically so that the priest can approach pastoral ministry with well-governed emotions.

137 At times, the struggles and wounds that emerge (sometimes, reemerge) in the pursuit of human formation are best addressed in the context of regular pastoral counseling by a therapist who adheres to the Catholic understanding of the human person, or at least understands the Catholic concept of the human person and will assist the priest in the context of that understanding. No priest should hesitate to take advantage of these resources when they are needed, because addressing his struggles courageously and growing in human maturity makes him a better instrument in the hands of the Lord for the service of souls.

FRATERNAL MEANS

138 During his visit in 2008, Pope Benedict XVI addressed the bishops of the United States as a body. It is noteworthy that the Holy Father chose that important occasion to offer these words about priestly fraternity and ongoing formation. "Each of us knows how important

priestly fraternity has been in our lives," he said. "That fraternity is not only a precious possession, but also an immense resource for the renewal of the priesthood and the raising up of new vocations."[111]

139 This "immense resource for the renewal of the priesthood"—that is, priestly fraternity—is first found in the gift of authentic friendship itself. Priestly friendships cannot settle for a shallow superficiality but must have the boldness to go deeper. By spending time together, getting to know one another, and sharing the gifts and struggles of priestly ministry, priests can be a source of tremendous strength for each other and a great means of human growth.

140 Friendships with brother priests make special demands on us and push us in unique ways. There is a transparency that comes with true friendship: being known by the other and wanting to be known, based upon a degree of earned trust and appropriate vulnerability. True priestly friendships offer the immeasurable gift of fraternal correction, a crucial source of self-knowledge and accountability, particularly for celibate priests, who do not have the natural correctives of a wife and family. The need for such correction has become all the clearer in the face of the clergy sexual abuse scandals of the last decades. It can only be speculated how many of those grave failures could have been avoided had wayward priests had priest friends to correct them in the first stages of their descent into deception and depravity.[112]

---

111   Pope Benedict XVI, "Responses to the Questions Posed by the Bishops," Meeting with the Bishops of the United States of America, National Shrine of the Immaculate Conception, Washington, DC, April 16, 2008, no. 3.

112   Many accused priests began abusing years after they were ordained, at times of increased job stress, social isolation, and decreased contact with peers. Generally, few structures such as psychological and professional counseling were readily available to assist them with the difficulties they experienced. Many priests let go of the practice of spiritual direction after only a few years of ordained ministry. See John Jay College Research Team, *The Causes and Context of Sexual Abuse of Minors by Catholic Priests in the United States*, 1950-2010 (Washington, DC: USCCB, 2011), 5.

141 Humble reception of fraternal correction is only part of the relationship. A priest must recognize his responsibility to provide fraternal correction to brother priests. In circumstances that involve serious threat to health and safety, if the priest receiving fraternal correction does not take measures to address the problematic behavior, then the brother priest has an obligation to go beyond the immediate relationship and advise diocesan officials of his concerns. Far from betraying friendship, this difficult act expresses true fraternal love.

142 Another important fraternal means for ongoing growth in human formation can be found in rectory living. Too often rectories are reduced to places where priests share a common residence and little more. They miss out on opportunities for mutual affection and support. At times the lack of fraternity can even intensify the loneliness of those whose only communion is physical proximity. All members of a rectory, especially the pastor, have the responsibility to ensure that it is a true Christian home, a place where each member feels at ease and where they enjoy periods of shared time, common prayer, and meals in common. Such a rectory often becomes a center of fraternity for priests who live alone, as well as a powerful means of growth in many human virtues such as patience, hospitality, generosity, humility, sincerity, personal discipline, and responsibility.[113] Also, clear separation of office and personal space can facilitate a healthy rectory life.

Episcopal Means

143 As spiritual fathers, diocesan bishops can foster the human growth of priests in many ways. One of the most important is by modeling, initiating, and encouraging priestly fraternity in their own lives

---

113   See DMLP, no. 39.

through their personal witness of friendship and by encouraging the fraternal groups that can provide so much support for priests. Diocesan bishops have another unique opportunity to promote the human formation of priests by making well-considered rectory assignments, giving attention not only to the abilities of the priests in question but also their capacity to live together.

144 In addition, diocesan bishops might consider hosting study days and convocations to address elements of human formation such as affective maturity, temperance with the Internet, the gift of celibacy, the fostering of better friendships, the use of accountability software, information about medical assistance and healthy living, and the helpful counseling services of faithful Catholic psychologists. Of equal importance, diocesan bishops can promote the human formation of their priests by making resources available to priests in need, especially the counseling services of faithful Catholic psychologists.

CHAPTER FOUR

SPIRITUAL FORMATION

145 In the final hours of his earthly ministry, Jesus spoke with a quiet intensity to the Apostles in the upper room. It was his "last testament" before undergoing his Passion and death. Among those final words, none were more intimate and profound than his earnest desire for their friendship: "I no longer call you slaves, because a slave does not know what his master is doing. I have called you friends, because I have told you everything I have heard from my Father. It was not you who chose me, but I who chose you and appointed you to go and bear fruit that will remain, so that whatever you ask the Father in my name he may give you" (Jn 15:15-16).

146 Jesus spoke these words to his Apostles at the Last Supper, traditionally understood as the origin of Holy Orders. "I have called you friends," he said. In saying it to them, he said it to all Christians of all times, and in a particular way to us priests. Jesus wants more from us than our service; he wants our friendship. He wants our heart. It is the one gift that we alone can give him.

147 A true friend is, according to ancient wisdom, "another self." The ancient wisdom is fulfilled quite literally in a priest's friendship with Jesus. Priests are, after all, explicitly called to be "another self" of Jesus—an *alter Christus*—for the people we serve. As we grow in friendship with the Lord, those bonds of charity permeate more and more of our lives. His good becomes our good, his thoughts our thoughts, his aspirations our aspirations. When he rejoices, we rejoice. When he weeps over another Jerusalem, we do so as well. We have made his ambitions our own.[114]

---

114 "In this his specific Christological identity the priest must be aware that his life is a mystery totally grafted onto the mystery of Christ and of the Church in a new way, and that this engages him totally

148 We must not forget that our friendship with Jesus as a priest—however close—rests on a prior foundation. Baptism is our rebirth in grace; it plants the seeds of the theological virtues. Through Baptism we are fashioned into children of God, and there is no greater honor on earth.[115] "For you I am a bishop," St. Augustine famously said, "[but] with you, after all, I am a Christian. The first is the name of an office undertaken, the second a name of a grace."[116] The role of spiritual formation is to draw us ever more deeply into the personal relationship with the Lord that is the birthright of every Christian—and the particular desire of Jesus for every priest.

149 Note, too, that Jesus called them friends and then appointed them "to go and bear fruit that will remain" (Jn 15:16). The priest's friendship with Christ finds its fulfillment in spiritual generativity. Because we exercise our fatherhood in the order of grace, it follows that our spiritual formation as priests takes on a special importance. As priests, we nurture a relationship with the Lord not only for our personal growth in sanctity, then, but also for the benefit of our priestly ministry. Our apostolic fruit will be reaped in direct proportion to the depth of our interior life.

MARKERS OF THE SPIRITUAL DIMENSION
Awareness of God's Love

150 Our personal relationship with the Father is not unlike that of natural children. Parents do not expect a personal response from a newborn

---

in the pastoral ministry and gives sense to his life." DMLP, no. 6.

115   "The ministerial priesthood conferred by the sacrament of holy orders and the common or 'royal' priesthood of the faithful, which differ essentially and not only in degree (Second Vatican Council, *Lumen Gentium*, no. 10), are ordered one to the other—for each in its own way derives from the one priesthood of Christ. Indeed, the ministerial priesthood does not of itself signify a greater degree of holiness with regard to the common priesthood of the faithful; through it Christ gives to priests, in the Spirit, a particular gift so that they can help the People of God to exercise faithfully and fully the common priesthood which it has received." PDV, no. 17.

116   St. Augustine, "Sermon 340—On the Anniversary of His Ordination," in *The Works of Saint Augustine: A Translation for the 21st Century*, pt. 3, vol. 9, *Sermons 306-340A* on the Saints, ed. John E. Rotelle, trans. Edmund Hill (Hyde Park, NY: New City Press, 1994), 292.

child, because the infant is not yet capable of it. Eventually, though, the child grows and begins to grasp the depth of his or her parents' love and starts to respond with love. That is the moment when love becomes reciprocal, even if the child cannot yet respond with the full freedom of an adult. In our life of faith, there comes a point when we are no longer infants—when we begin to grasp, however partially, God's love for us. "When I was a child," St. Paul tells the Corinthians, "I used to talk as a child, think as a child, reason as a child; when I became a man, I put aside childish things. . . . At present I know partially; then I shall know fully, as I am fully known" (1 Cor 13:11-12).

151   A key marker of the spiritual maturity of the priest is therefore the awareness of God's love. The priest's growth in the interior life hinges largely on the firm conviction that he is the object of God's particular, personal, loving care. By embracing this relationship to the Father, in communion with the Holy Spirit, the priest grasps this identity as a "son in the Son." That identity, in turn, enkindles his mission in life, his life of discipleship, his apostolate with others, and ultimately his priestly mission as a spiritual father. The priest is able "through divine filiation to experience the paternal providence that never abandons its children. If this is true for each Christian it is equally true that the priest, by virtue of the consecration received with the sacrament of Holy Orders, is placed in a particular and special relationship with the Father, with the Son and with the Holy Spirit."[117]

UNION WITH THE SACRIFICE OF CHRIST

152   Of central importance to a priest's interior growth is union with Christ in his sacrifice on the Cross. Christ is the innocent Lamb of God who, as the High Priest of our faith, offers himself in a holocaust

---

117   DMLP, no. 3.

of love. His sacrificial offering and his priesthood are inseparable.[118] Those who are conformed to Christ the Head of the Church—that is to Christ the Priest—are thereby also conformed to Christ the Victim.[119] Priests who embrace their own struggles and sacrifices as opportunities to share, however slightly, in the Lord's Passion are tapping into a deep reservoir in their priestly vocation. Like the priest St. Paul says, a priest is "filling up what is lacking in the afflictions of Christ on behalf of his body, which is the church, of which I am a minister in accordance with God's stewardship given to me" (Col 1:24-25). Union with the Passion of Christ is thus the foundation of an authentic Christian asceticism, which is an important marker of spiritual depth in a Christian disciple and priest.[120]

PURSUIT OF HOLINESS

153 In the rite of presbyteral ordination, the presiding bishop exhorts the ordinands: "Understand, therefore, what you do, and imitate what you celebrate; as celebrants of the mystery of the Lord's Death and Resurrection, may you strive to put to death whatever is sinful within you and to walk in newness of life."[121] An important marker of spiritual formation is therefore the committed resolution to grow in

---

118 "Through the ministry of priests, the spiritual sacrifice of the faithful is made perfect in union with the sacrifice of Christ, the sole Mediator. Through the hands of priests and in the name of the whole Church, the Lord's sacrifice is offered in the Eucharist in an unbloody and sacramental manner until He Himself returns. The ministry of priests is directed toward this work and is perfected in it. For their ministry, which takes its start from the gospel message, derives its power and force from the sacrifice of Christ." PO, no. 2.

119 "By virtue of this consecration brought about by the outpouring of the Spirit in the sacrament of holy orders, the spiritual life of the priest is marked, molded and characterized by the way of thinking and acting proper to Jesus Christ, head and shepherd of the Church, and which are summed up in his pastoral charity." PDV, no. 21.

120 "Ongoing formation will help such priests to keep alive the conviction—which they themselves have inculcated in the faithful—that they continue to be active members for the building up of the Church, especially by virtue of their union with the suffering Christ and with so many other brothers and sisters in the Church who are sharing in the Lord's passion, reliving Paul's spiritual experience when he said, 'I rejoice in my sufferings for your sake, and in my flesh I complete what is lacking in Christ's afflictions for the sake of his body, that is, the Church' (Col 1:24)." PDV, no. 77.

121 Roman Pontifical, *Ordination of a Bishop, of Priests, and of Deacons*, English trans. of second typical ed. (Washington, DC: USCCB, 2021), no. 123.

holiness, to embrace the "newness of life" promised in the Gospel.[122] For a priest, true growth in holiness always produces greater pastoral charity. The priest can give no greater gift to his people than his own resolve to grow in sanctity. Holiness is the fruit both of grace and of one's free and generous efforts. As St. John Neumann fervently prayed at his first Mass, "O God, give me holiness!"[123]

154 A holy life is made up of many elements. It presumes, for example, rightly ordered faith and intellectual honesty. It includes moral integrity and fidelity to the law of God. It is sustained by the sacraments, an active life of prayer, and the presence of God, including a love for silence and solitude. It relies upon and fosters a supernatural outlook, seeing one's life, world, and relationships through the lens of faith, that is, from the perspective of eternity.

155 The Second Vatican Council taught, "Therefore, since every priest in his own way represents the person of Christ Himself, he is also enriched with special grace. Thus, serving the people committed to him and the entire People of God, he can more properly imitate the perfection of Him whose part he takes. Thus, too, the weakness of human flesh can be healed by the holiness of Him who has become for our sake a high priest 'holy, innocent, undefiled, set apart from sinners' (Heb 7:26)."[124] In light of a priest's particular call to draw souls to Christ, his holiness will also be distinguished by his efforts to keep God, rather than his own preferences and ego, at the center of his life.

---

122 "Ongoing formation is a requirement that begins and develops from the moment of receiving the Sacrament of Holy Orders, with which the priest is not only 'consecrated' by the Father, 'sent' by the Son, but also 'animated' by the Holy Spirit." DMLP, no. 87.
123 St. John Neumann, quoted in "Oh God, Give Me Holiness," The Redemptorists, January 5, 2012.
124 PO, no. 12. See also CIC, c. 276, for specific means of growth in holiness.

156 Commenting on St. John's Gospel, St. Augustine captured this aspect of priestly holiness well. The shepherds of Christ's flock must never indulge in self-love; if they do they will be tending the sheep not as Christ's but as their own. St. Augustine wrote, "This is the vice that must be most guarded against by those who feed Christ's sheep, lest they seek what is their own rather than what is Jesus Christ's and turn to the uses of their own desires those for whom Christ's blood was shed."[125]

FIDELITY TO THE CHURCH

157 Obedience in the life of a priest requires far more than mere compliance to the will of a superior. It is founded on trust that God's plan is always better than his own, because it is the fruit of the Father's paternal care for each soul. "Are not two sparrows sold for a small coin?" Jesus asked. "Yet not one of them falls to the ground without your Father's knowledge" (Mt 10:29). For the priest in particular, obedience springs from the eucharistic sacrifice, in which he unites his own self-offering to Jesus' perfect self-offering to the Father. The priest freely offers to God his own plans and preferences for the sake of the Gospel and orients his will toward faithfully obeying legitimate authority within the Church, so that he can be a more effective instrument for the good of souls.

158 The priest of Christ, whose bride is the Church, is uniquely called to love and respect her in a spousal manner. Only through the Church can the priest generate spiritual children; indeed it is through her that he receives his very office. A priest who undercuts the Church's authority through disobedience or infidelity commits a grave injustice to the people he serves and poisons the very wellsprings of his own

---

125 St. Augustine, "Homily 123 on John 21:12-19," in *The Works of Saint Augustine: A Translation for the 21st Century*, pt. 3, vol. 13, *Homilies on the Gospel of John* 41-124, ed. Allan D. Fitzgerald, trans. Edmund Hill (Hyde Park, NY: New City Press, 2020), 533.

priesthood. "Loyalty toward Christ," the Second Vatican Council affirmed, "can never be divorced from loyalty toward His Church."[126] Ecclesial fidelity is, then, a third marker of spiritual formation.

159 The mature priest pays special attention to his attitude toward the Church—not as the Church is in glory, not as he wishes it were now, not as he imagines it once was, but as the Church actually is here, today. He will love the Church as a mother and a teacher and embrace church teachings with gratitude and humility. He will faithfully convey the Catholic faith to his people comprehensively, accurately, and with conviction. He will fulfill liturgical and other norms without needing to put his own idiosyncratic stamp on them.[127] He will cultivate piety and respect toward the pope as well as his own diocesan bishop and the College of Bishops. In loving the Church, he loves all her members, both those on earth and those in glory or in purgatory. He nourishes in himself a deep love for Our Lady and the saints, the angels, and the departed souls who are being prepared for their new life of glory.[128]

160 In today's confused and fractured age, the priest must strive to be an agent of unity in the Church—not with the false irenicism that ignores important challenges or papers over meaningful differences and fissures in the Church, but rather with a genuine desire to

---

126 PO, no. 14. Regarding the participation of the priest in the spousal nature of Christ with the Church, see DMLP, nos. 13-14. Regarding the relationship of the priest's spiritual life to pastoral charity, see PDV, nos. 22-24.

127 See CIC, c. 846 §1.

128 "[St. Padre Pio] loved the Church, with the many problems the Church has, with so many adversities, with so many sinners. Because the Church is holy, she is the Bride of Christ, but we, the children of the Church, are all sinners—some big ones!—but he loved the Church as she was, he did not destroy her with the tongue, as it is the fashion to do now. No! He loved her. He who loves the Church knows how to forgive, because he knows that he himself is a sinner and is in need of God's forgiveness. He knows how to arrange things, because the Lord wants to arrange things well but always with forgiveness: one cannot live an entire life accusing, accusing, accusing the Church. Whose is the office of the accuser! The devil! And those who spend their life accusing, accusing, accusing, are—I will not say children, because the devil does not have any—but friends, cousins, relatives of the devil. And no, this is not good, flaws must be indicated so they can be corrected, but at the moment that flaws are noted, flaws are denounced, one loves the Church. Without love, that is of the devil." Francis, Greeting to the Archdiocese of Benevento, February 20, 2019.

promote authentic bonds of charity and understanding among Catholics. A priest who is spiritually mature strives to rise above the din of competing ideologies and overwrought websites in order to remain focused on what is important. He does not shy away from exposing sin, error, or corruption, but neither does he take morbid delight in doing so. He is a man who genuinely desires the good of all, whatever their past, and who receives with warmth and affection all those seeking Christ. He strives to emulate the Good Shepherd, who seeks out the one lost and straying sheep, however far it may have wandered.[129]

MEANS OF SPIRITUAL FORMATION
Personal Means

161 The personal means of spiritual formation are the behaviors and habits that allow the priest to grow in holiness, so that souls entrusted to him may be drawn to Christ. Just as he should avoid near occasions of sin, where he is more likely to fall into immorality, so he should seek out occasions of grace, where he is more likely to fall in love with the Lord. The personal means of spiritual formation are those occasions of grace that draw the priest into deeper relationship with the Lord.

162 For a priest, indeed for all Catholics, the most important means of formation is the daily celebration of Holy Mass.[130] The Second

---

129 "Priests have been placed in the midst of the laity to lead them to the unity of charity, that they may 'love one another with fraternal charity, anticipating one another with honor' (Rom 12:10). It is their task, therefore, to reconcile differences of mentality in such a way that no one will feel himself a stranger in the community of the faithful. Priests are defenders of the common good, with which they are charged in the name of the bishop. At the same time, they are strenuous defenders of the truth, lest the faithful be tossed about by every wind of opinion. To their special concern are committed those who have fallen away from the use of the sacraments, or perhaps even from the faith. As good shepherds, they should not cease from going after them." PO, no. 9.

130 See CIC, cc. 276 §2, 2°, 904, and 906. For the priest, the daily celebration of the Holy Mass has irreplaceable value—it is the "source and summit" (see LG, no. 11; PO, no. 18) of the priestly life—even if it is not possible to have the faithful present. In this regard Pope Benedict XVI teaches: "To this end I join the Synod Fathers in recommending 'the daily celebration of Mass, even when the faithful are not present.' This recommendation is consistent with the objectively infinite value of every celebration of the Eucharist, and is motivated by the Mass's unique spiritual fruitfulness. If celebrated in a faith-filled and attentive way, Mass is formative in the deepest sense of the word, since it fosters the priest's configuration to Christ and strengthens him in his vocation." Benedict XVI, *Sacramentum*

Vatican Council taught that the Eucharist "is the summit toward which the activity of the Church is directed; at the same time it is the font from which all her power flows."[131] That is true not only of the Church, but of the priest too. In the reverent celebration of Mass every day, the priest is himself nourished at the font of grace and offers to God all the fruits of his priestly activity. The Mass is the source and the summit of his priesthood. St. John Vianney stated bluntly that the "reason why priests are remiss in their personal lives is that they do not offer the Sacrifice with attention and piety."[132] If a priest wishes to grow in his interior life, he can find no better place to start than by offering the Holy Mass with greater love.[133]

163 Closely allied to the Mass and flowing from it are two other important personal means of spiritual growth. The first is the Liturgy of the Hours, through which the priest gives voice to the prayer of the Church and takes part in the ceaseless praise of God through the centuries.[134] Through these prayers, priests "extend to the different hours of the day the praise and thanksgiving of the Eucharistic celebration. . . . [offered] in the name of the Church on behalf of the whole people entrusted to them and indeed for the whole world."[135] Giving the breviary more time and attention, even if he sometimes struggles to align his emotions to the words, is another way, ready at hand, for the priest to grow in spiritual depth.

Caritatis (On the Eucharist as the Source and Summit of the Church's Life and Mission), February 22, 2007, no. 80. See also DMLP, no. 67. Reflection on and study of the *General Instruction of the Roman Missal*, especially nos. 78-79, can deepen the spiritual fruitfulness for the priest.

131 Second Vatican Council, *Sacrosanctum Concilium (Constitution on the Sacred Liturgy)*, no. 10, in *The Documents of Vatican II*, ed. Walter M. Abbott (New York: Corpus Books, 1966). Subsequently cited as SC.

132 St. John Vianney, quoted in St. John XXIII, *Sacerdotii Nostri Primordia (On St. John Vianney)*, August 1, 1959, no. 58.

133 See PO, no. 13.

134 See CIC, c. 276 §2, 3°.

135 PO, no. 5.

164 In addition to the Liturgy of the Hours, Adoration of the Blessed Sacrament is a choice fruit of the Mass that countless Catholics have found to be an indispensable element of their spiritual growth.[136] Although many priests continue to nourish their prayer through regular Eucharistic Adoration, others struggle to keep alive their eucharistic devotion, perhaps due to the dangers of overfamiliarity. In such cases, reigniting a love for the Eucharistic Lord is a path toward renewed spiritual growth.

165 After the Mass and its principal fruits, another category of occasions of grace includes all the personal practices of piety that enrich a priest's spiritual life. Foremost is the habit of personal prayer, specifically mental prayer or meditation.[137] In the busy schedule of a priest, he must jealously procure and defend intentional time away and jealously defend intentional time of solitude with the Lord.[138] An abundance of responsibilities and a long task list do not excuse a single priest from daily personal prayer. St. Francis de Sales, talking to priests, insisted that they make a thirty-minute meditation every day, "except when we are busy—then we need an hour."[139]

166 Once he sets aside the amount of time, ideally an hour, of mental prayer each day, there is the question of making good use of the time. Many have found the practice of *lectio divina* to be of immense help. Reading the Scriptures slowly and reverently, listening for the guidance of the Spirit, responding in love, and resting in contemplation—the *lectio divina* is a time-honored way to hear and

---

136 "The centrality of the Eucharist must appear not only in the worthy and deeply felt celebration of the Sacrifice, but also in frequent adoration of the Sacrament of the Altar so the priest may be seen as a model for the flock also in devout attention and assiduous meditation in the presence of the Lord in the tabernacle." DMLP, no. 68.

137 See CIC, c. 276 §2, 5°.

138 "Therefore, the fundamental priority for each priest is his personal relationship with Christ through the abundance of moments of silence and prayer for cultivating and deepening his relationship with the living person of the Lord Jesus." DMLP, no. 51.

139 St. Francis de Sales, quoted in USCCB, *United States Catholic Catechism for Adults* (Washington, DC: USCCB, 2006), 463.

speak to God.[140] A complementary approach to mental prayer is to dwell on each of the four acts of prayer: adoration, contrition, thanksgiving, and supplication (easily remembered with the acronym ACTS). Using this template, the priest can speak to the Lord in his own words of love: adoring and praising him, expressing contrition for sins, thanking Christ for the blessings in his life, and asking the Lord to supply the needs of his priestly ministry, of the people entrusted to his care, and of the whole world.

167   Apart from mental prayer, every master of the spiritual life has recommended the practice of spiritual reading. Careful reading of spiritual works puts the priest in touch with the great doctrinal and mystical Tradition of the Church, informs his mind, and feeds his prayer. Especially recommended for spiritual reading are time-honored classics such as the writings of saints and especially the Doctors and Fathers of the Church.

168   A rich devotional life also nourishes the interior life of a priest. Particularly important are the great devotions to Divine Mercy and the Sacred Heart of Jesus as well as the principal devotions to the Blessed Virgin, including the Holy Rosary and the Total Consecration to Mary taught by St. Louis de Montfort. When St. John, the Beloved Disciple, took Mary "into his home" (Jn 19:25-27), it was more than an act of kindness. Doing so completely changed the young priest's

---

140   The priestly vocation demands that one be consecrated "in the truth." Jesus states this clearly with regard to his disciples: "Consecrate them in the truth. Your word is truth. As you sent me into the world, so I sent them into the world" (Jn 17:17-18). The disciples in a certain sense were "thus drawn deep within God by being immersed in the word of God. The word of God is, so to speak, the bath which purifies them, the creative power which transforms them into God's own being" Benedict XVI, Homily, 2009 Chrism Mass, April 9, 2009. And Christ himself is God's Word made flesh (see Jn 1:14)—"the truth" (Jn 14:6). Thus Jesus' prayer to the Father, "Consecrate them in the truth," means in the deepest sense: "Make them one with me, Christ. Bind them to me. Draw them into me. . . . there is only one priest of the New Covenant, Jesus Christ himself." Benedict XVI, Homily, 2009 Chrism Mass. "Priests need to grow constantly in their awareness of this reality." Benedict XVI, *Verbum Domini (On the Word of God in the Life and Mission of the Church)*, September 30, 2010, no. 80.

life. Mary became an integral part of John's daily affairs, his choices, and his aspirations. She was invited into every part of his life and his heart. John set the pattern for every priest.

169 In recent times the role of St. Joseph has become more prominent in the life of the Church and also in the lives of priests. St. Joseph—so close to the Incarnate Word and to his Holy Mother, as the protector of Jesus and of Mary—has much to teach priests who have been called, like him, to fatherhood in the order of grace.[141] He is a great friend, intercessor, and guide in one's priestly ministry. In addition to Our Lady and St. Joseph, every priest has personal devotions to cherished saints, heavenly patrons, and the angels, especially his guardian angel. These bonds of love to friends in heaven nourish the life of faith and contribute greatly to spiritual formation.

170 Practices of personal prayer and devotion are not intended to be confined to actual moments of prayer; rather, they should overflow into the rest of a priest's life. Time spent in prayer is the source of warmth that raises the spiritual temperature of the entire day, so to speak, helping the priest to live in God's presence more habitually. That habit is reinforced by regular recourse to aspirations throughout the day, spiritual communions, and small self-denials and sacrifices that concretely express the priest's love for God. Fostering the presence of God in his life also facilitates his discernment of spirits by which interior movements of the soul, such as thoughts, feelings, and desires, are understood and acted upon appropriately. Also being

---

141 "Joseph's attitude encourages us to accept and welcome others as they are, without exception, and to show special concern for the weak, for God chooses what is weak (see 1 Cor 1:27). He is the 'Father of orphans and protector of widows' (Ps 68:6), who commands us to love the stranger in our midst. I like to think that it was from Saint Joseph that Jesus drew inspiration for the parable of the prodigal son and the merciful father (see Lk 15:11-32)." Francis, *Patris Corde (On the 150th Anniversary of the Proclamation of St. Joseph as Patron of the Universal Church)*, December 8, 2020, no. 4.

attentive to and affirming the piety and pious practices of the people he serves can enrich his own spiritual growth.[142]

171 Other personal means of growing in the spiritual life include the regular study of Sacred Scripture, a daily examination of conscience, an annual retreat,[143] regular confession,[144] consistent spiritual direction,[145] and periods of more intensive spiritual formation, such as days of recollection, spiritual workshops, and individual "desert days," that is, days set aside to be alone and quiet with the Lord.

172 All personal means of spiritual growth presented thus far configure the heart of the priest more closely to the heart of Jesus Christ and culminate in pastoral charity. A reciprocal relationship exists between growth in intimacy with Christ, especially through the Eucharist, and growth in participation in the pastoral charity of Christ, the gift of oneself to the Church.[146]

---

142 "In this way, future priests will acquire familiarity with the 'popular spirituality' that they will be called upon to discern, guide and accept out of pastoral charity and effectiveness." *Ratio Fundamentalis*, no. 114, quoting St. Paul VI, *Evangelii Nuntiandi*, no. 48.

143 "More specifically, it is hoped that each priest, perhaps during periodical retreats, would draw up a concrete plan of personal life in concord with his spiritual director. The following elements may be suggested: (1) daily meditation on the Word or a mystery of the faith; (2) daily personal encounter with Jesus in the Eucharist, in addition to devote celebration of Mass and frequent Confession; (3) Marian devotion (Rosary, consecration or entrustment, intimate colloquy); (4) a period of doctrinal formation and study of the history of the saints; (5) due rest; (6) renewed commitment in putting into practice the indications of one's Bishop and verification of one's convinced adhesion to the *Magisterium* and to ecclesiastical discipline; (7) attention to priestly communion, friendship and fraternity. Likewise to be deepened are other aspects such as the administration of one's time and goods, work, and the importance of working with others." DMLP, no. 94 (emphasis original). See also CIC, c. 276 §2, 2° and 4°.

144 See CIC, c. 276 §2, 5°.

145 "By placing the formation of their soul in the hands of a wise confrere—the instrument of the Holy Spirit—they will develop, as of their first steps in the ministry, their awareness of the importance of not journeying in solitude along the ways of the spiritual life and pastoral commitment. In making use of this efficacious means of formation so well tried and proven in the Church, priests are to exercise complete liberty in choosing the person who may guide them." DMLP, no. 73.

146 "The internal principle, the force which animates and guides the spiritual life of the priest inasmuch as he is configured to Christ the head and shepherd, is pastoral charity, as a participation in Jesus Christ's own pastoral charity. . . . The essential content of this pastoral charity is the gift of self, the total gift of self to the Church, following the example of Christ. . . . the priest's pastoral charity not only flows from the Eucharist but finds in the celebration of the Eucharist its highest realization—just as it is from the Eucharist that he receives the grace and obligation to give his whole life a 'sacrificial' dimension." PDV, no. 23.

FRATERNAL MEANS

173 Although the principal responsibility for spiritual formation rests on the shoulders of each priest, his personal efforts can be greatly enhanced by fraternal support. Of primary importance are Christ-centered friendships with other priests. It is difficult to overestimate the influence of brother priests who encourage and affirm each other in their spiritual practices, hold each other accountable as needed, and inspire one another to grow in holiness. They "seek to promote fraternal communion by giving and receiving—from priest to priest—the warmth of friendship, caring assistance, acceptance and fraternal correction."[147]

174 St. Basil the Great and St. Gregory Nazianzen were friends whose mutual affection and holy "competition" spurred both to ever-greater heights of holiness.[148] Priests today can enjoy that kind of friendship as well, with the spiritual fruits that flow from it. Even for friendships in the earlier stages, priests can very naturally begin to spend fraternal time together in prayer and ensure that spiritual topics, if not the exclusive content of their conversation, are at least not forbidden.

175 Priest friends can also contribute to each other's spiritual growth by coming together for more extensive periods of prayer. For instance, small groups of priests might consider taking a monthly or quarterly day of prayer at a local monastery, retreat center, or another place

---

147 DMLP, no. 36.
148 "We were impelled by equal hopes, in a pursuit obnoxious to envy, that of letters. Yet envy we knew not, and emulation was of service to us. We struggled, not each to gain the first place for himself, but to yield it to the other; for we made each other's reputation to be our own. . . . The sole business of both of us was virtue, and living for the hopes to come, having retired from this world, before our actual departure hence. With a view to this, were directed all our life and actions, under the guidance of the commandment, as we sharpened upon each other our weapons of virtue; and if this is not a great thing for me to say, being a rule and standard to each other, for the distinction between what was right and what was not." St. Gregory Nazianzen, *Oratio* 43: "Funeral Oration on the Great S. Basil, Bishop of Caesarea in Cappadocia," no. 20, in *Nicene and Post-Nicene Fathers*, 2nd series, vol. 7, eds. Philip Schaff and Henry Wace, trans. Charles Gordon Browne and James Edward Swallow (Buffalo, NY: Christian Literature Publishing Co., 1894).

of solitude. By sharing prayer together, they encourage each other in perseverance and offer a measure of accountability. Similarly, fraternal groups such as those in the Jesus Caritas tradition can encourage spiritual growth through spiritual conversation, periods of prayer, and sharing of graces and struggles.[149]

EPISCOPAL MEANS

176 Diocesan bishops and their diocesan resources can do much to promote the spiritual formation of priests.[150] One important way is by offering diocesan retreats and days of recollection. Finding suitable and engaging preachers is not always easy; and a diocesan bishop's personal attention to those choices, perhaps by personally inviting potential retreat masters, can motivate priests to attend. With the efficiency of modern travel, priests can also attend clergy retreats further afield without much difficulty. Identifying and encouraging these options, especially those aimed specifically at diocesan priests, can help them fulfill the canonical requirement that priests spend several days away in prayer annually.[151] In light of that expectation, diocesan bishops might also consider asking each priest yearly to identify when and where he plans to make his retreat.

177 On a more regular basis, diocesan bishops can cultivate the spiritual growth of priests by identifying and making available suitable

---

149 "Among the diverse forms of common life (residence, community at table, etc.), held in eminent pride of place is to be communal participation in liturgical prayer (see SC, nos. 26, 99; *Institutio Generalis Liturgiae Horarum*, no. 25). Its diverse modalities are to be encouraged according to possibilities and practical conditions, without necessarily transferring the albeit praiseworthy models proper to the religious life. Worthy of praise in particular are those associations which support priestly fraternity, holiness in the exercise of the ministry, and communion with the Bishop and the entire Church (see CIC, c. 278 §2; see also PDV, nos. 31, 68, 81)." DMLP, no. 39.

150 "In the present social context, the Bishop needs to remain particularly close to his flock and above all to his priests, showing a father's concern for their ascetic and spiritual difficulties, and providing them with appropriate support to encourage them in fidelity to their vocation and to the requirements of an exemplary life in the exercise of the ministry." St. John Paul II, *Pastores Gregis (On the Bishop, Servant of the Gospel of Jesus Christ for the Hope of the World)*, October 16, 2003, no. 21. See also *Apostolorum Successores*, no. 81.

151 See CIC, c. 276 §2, 4°.

confessors and spiritual directors. Meeting this need might mean offering formal training in spiritual direction for local, trusted priests or inviting outside priestly help from nearby dioceses or religious orders. For areas that are more sparsely populated, meeting this need might involve regional cooperation among adjacent dioceses. Remote spiritual direction can be a good option. Helping priests find good spiritual directors fosters their ongoing spiritual formation.[152] The diocesan bishop's personal witness of receiving spiritual direction himself is also invaluable, together with his regular encouragement that priests do the same.

178 In addition, priest study days and priest gatherings can always include some time in prayer, perhaps concelebration of Mass with the bishop, time in Adoration of the Eucharist, or celebration of the Liturgy of the Hours in common. These practices set a tone of prayerfulness for a presbyterate.

179 Last, to foster prayerful time away for priests, singly or in groups, some dioceses have made available a house of prayer. Such a refuge can offer priests a place to rest, pray, and detach from devices, email, social media, and other distractions so that they can focus more intentionally on their relationship with God—the goal of spiritual formation.

---

152   It can be difficult in some circumstances for a priest to find a spiritual director. In such cases, asking the Lord to provide and trusting in his providence are appropriate.

CHAPTER FIVE
INTELLECTUAL FORMATION

180 It is remarkable how much of Jesus' ministry was taken up in teaching. One might even say that the purpose of the Incarnation, after redemption itself, was to teach humanity how to embrace the Gospel. Jesus taught in sermons, in parables, and in actions. Mary and Joseph found him as a boy in the Temple, "sitting in the midst of the teachers, listening to them and asking them questions, and all who heard him were astounded at his understanding and his answers" (Lk 2:46-47). Throughout his public ministry, Jesus was teaching.

181 After his Resurrection, Jesus taught the disciples on the road to Emmaus. "Beginning with Moses and all the prophets, he interpreted to them what referred to him in all the scriptures" (Lk 24:27). That same Easter Sunday evening, he appeared to the disciples in the upper room and "opened their minds to understand the scriptures" (Lk 24:45). St. Luke began his Acts of the Apostles by commenting on "all that Jesus did and taught until the day he was taken up" (Acts 1:1-2). Jesus was constantly engaged in the intellectual formation of his disciples.

182 Forming the intellect is important for every Christian because the mind is like the tiller of a boat. With a small shift it can change the entire direction of a life. The last century of history, with its hundreds of millions of dead at the feet of pernicious ideologies, stands as a bleak testament to the power and importance of the mind. It has never been more urgent to pass on the life-giving message of the Gospel.

183 A sound intellectual formation also preserves the mind from the tyranny of impulse and an unmoored imagination. As has been said many times before, without doctrine the Christian becomes a mere sentimentalist. "From the age of fifteen," St. John Henry Newman wrote, "dogma has been the fundamental principle of my religion: I know no other religion; I cannot enter into the idea of any other sort of religion; religion, as a mere sentiment, is to me a dream and a mockery."[153]

184 Perhaps most importantly, intellectual formation nourishes our love for God. No one can love the unknown, and the one who loves can never know enough about the beloved. Our relationship with God is no exception. We learn directly about him through the Scriptures and the teaching of the Church. This study is the work of both grace and nature, culminating in a conversion of heart, a genuine renewal of mind. "Do not conform yourselves to this age," St. Paul wrote to the Romans, "but be transformed by the renewal of your mind, that you may discern what is the will of God, what is good and pleasing and perfect" (Rom 12:2).

185 We also learn about God indirectly through the wider panorama of intellectual formation. In a sense, every field of human knowledge can give us glimpses of the divine, whether we are captured by the beauty of a sunset, the stunning majesty of faraway galaxies, or the intricate beauty of organic cells—whether we are studying the great works of literature or music or sorting through the complexities of human history. For believers who know that nothing is outside the Providence of God, everything we learn becomes an occasion to find him in new ways.

---

153   St. John Henry Newman, Apologia Pro Vita Sua, 1865, chap. 2.

186   The intellect is made to grasp reality and penetrate its meaning. Since no part of our life falls outside its influence, ongoing intellectual formation is a thread that binds the four dimensions of priestly formation together. In the human dimension, for instance, study is a way for us priests to broaden our perspective, stimulate creativity, generate enthusiasm for new ideas, and encourage healthy habits.

187   In the spiritual dimension, study increases our knowledge of God and the things of God, fostering a habit of theology in the widest sense, that is, seeing everything from a supernatural point of view. In disciplining the mind to focus, study promotes interiority as well as the self-control needed to live a regular plan of life, including the spiritual practices that are the "occasions of grace" described in chapter four. By providing matter for prayer and opening a space for solitude and quiet, study can contribute to a more contemplative life for us as priests.

188   In the pastoral dimension, study gives rise to new ideas for our preaching, teaching, and counsel as priests. Much of the intellectual matter for our pastoral mission arises from steady growth in the intellectual life.[154] It educates us in the doctrinal richness and spiritual Tradition of the Catholic faith and gives us something to hand on. It ensures that we remain faithful to the mind of the Church, as St. Paul did when he conferred with the Apostles in Jerusalem to ensure that he "might not be running, or have run, in vain" (Gal 2:2). On a more personal level, regular study offers a healthy balance against the practical realities of priestly ministry and helps us integrate those realities into a larger vision that can keep our daily ministry fresh and dynamic.

---

154   "Therefore, the priest, with the help of the Holy Spirit, the study of the Word of God in the Scriptures, and in light of both Tradition and the *Magisterium*, discovers the richness of the Word to be proclaimed to the ecclesial community entrusted to his care." DMLP, no. 10, emphasis original.

189 Intellectual formation is, then, not only for those priests who happen to demonstrate a more academic bent. It is a dimension of life important for every priest and one that will have a decisive influence on our personal maturity, interior life, and apostolic ministry.

MARKERS OF THE INTELLECTUAL DIMENSION
CATECHETICAL AND THEOLOGICAL COMPETENCE

190 The first and most obvious marker of intellectual formation for a priest is a deep knowledge of the faith. Much of the foundation for this marker will have occurred in seminary studies. There are two primary characteristics of the priest who is intellectually well formed. The first is objective, namely the doctrinal content of his formation. He should have a mastery of the teachings of the faith "drawn primarily from reading and meditating on the sacred Scriptures. But it should also be fruitfully nourished by a study of the Holy Fathers and Doctors and other annals of tradition. In addition, [so] that they may be able to provide proper answers to the questions discussed by the men of this age, priests should be well acquainted with the documents of the Church's teaching authority and especially of Councils and the Roman Pontiffs. They should consult, too, the best, approved writers in theological science."[155] The priest must know the teachings articulated in the *Catechism of the Catholic Church*. Beyond that, he should have an awareness of the theological background of those teachings and the overall historical arc of theology through the centuries. A faithful priest strives for ever more precision and clarity in his grasp of theological ideas and discourse.

191 The second characteristic of intellectual formation is subjective, namely a priest's fidelity to Catholic teachings.[156] The priest—entrusted with

---

155 PO, no. 19.
156 "The awareness of the absolute need to 'remain' faithful to and anchored in the Word of God and Tradition in order to be true disciples of Christ and know the truth (see Jn 8:31-32) has always ac-

handing on the precious Deposit of Faith—should stand out for his confident adherence to true doctrine.[157] The humility of intellectual assent proper to all official Catholic teachers and preachers is far from passivity, servitude, or timidity. Such assent is rather a vigorous application of one's intellect, placing it at the service of revealed truth. It is, in fact, the highest exercise of the mind, which, like all our faculties, is made to glorify its Creator. "The assent of faith, engaging the intellect and will," Fides et Ratio reminds us, "does not destroy but perfects the free will of each believer who deep within welcomes what has been revealed."[158] By probing the limits of human understanding, especially the fields of knowledge unveiled by God's own Revelation, the human intellect finds its most sublime purpose and its greatest achievement.[159]

ENGAGEMENT WITH THE WORLD

192 The second marker of intellectual formation is broader than the first. The first deals specifically with the content of faith; the second deals with the content of human learning. The Second Vatican Council taught, "The Church has always had the duty of scrutinizing the signs of the times and of interpreting them in the light of the Gospel."[160] The priest who is well formed intellectually engages the contemporary world, with all its possibilities and all its faults, with

---

companied the history of the priestly spirituality, and was also reiterated in an authoritative manner by the Second Vatican Ecumenical Council." DMLP, no. 62.

157 "Above all for contemporary society marked as it is in many countries by theoretical and practical materialism, subjectivism and cultural relativism, it is necessary for the Gospel to be presented as 'the power of God for the salvation of everyone who believes' (Rm 1:16). Priests, recalling that 'the faith comes from what is preached, and what is preached comes from the word of Christ' (Rm 10:17), will devote their every energy to correspond to this mission, which is primary in their ministry. Indeed, they are not only witnesses, but heralds and transmitters of the faith (see CIC, cc. 757, 762, 776)." DMLP, no. 62.

158 St. John Paul II, *Fides et Ratio (On the Relationship Between Faith and Reason)*, September 14, 1998, no. 75. See also CIC, c. 750.

159 "Although he made much of the supernatural character of faith, the Angelic Doctor did not overlook the importance of its reasonableness; indeed he was able to plumb the depths and explain the meaning of this reasonableness. Faith is in a sense an 'exercise of thought'; and human reason is neither annulled nor debased in assenting to the contents of faith, which are in any case attained by way of free and informed choice." St. John Paul II, *Fides et Ratio*, no. 43.

160 GS, no. 4.

calmness and poise. He has a healthy love for secular knowledge, both cultural and scientific, and cultivates an interest in social trends, public affairs, and his own intellectual passions. These are some ways that the priest can read "the signs of the times" and, as the Council taught, address them in "in the light of the Gospel."

193   A wider intellectual vision also enables a priest to articulate the Catholic faith in a way that is beautiful and compelling.[161] Moreover, he can defend the truth of Catholic teaching because he has considered opposing arguments seriously, recognizing in many of them a well-intentioned desire to seek the truth. He assumes neither malice nor irrationality in those who object to Catholic doctrine. His presentation of the Gospel, in other words, satisfies the deepest longings of his people, because he has felt those longings himself. This mature open-mindedness, shared by all great apologists through the centuries, most effectively clears away others' intellectual obstacles to belief and reinforces his own confidence in the truth taught by the Church.

Thirst for Intellectual Growth

194   The third marker of the intellectual dimension is perhaps also the most difficult to articulate. It is an interior hunger for the truth, not as a private hobby or as an idiosyncratic and academic curiosity, but from a deep desire to know ever more about the One we love. This marker recognizes that intellectual formation is, like the other areas of formation, not a static achievement. Knowing our Catechism is not enough, nor is proficiency in the theological and mystical tradition. An atheist could memorize the Bible, the *Catechism*, and

---

161   "Since . . . human culture and the sacred sciences are making new advances, priests are urged to develop their knowledge of divine and human affairs aptly and uninterruptedly. In this way they will prepare themselves more appropriately to undertake discussions with their contemporaries." PO, no. 19.

the theological masters and still not have this interior longing to know more about our beloved God.

195 This final marker of formation, then, is not an intellectual goal but rather the fruit of a relationship. As the priest gives himself more generously to God, the Father plants in the priest's mind the seeds of a desire to know him still more profoundly.[162] This desire is the most precious sign of being "transformed by the renewal" of the mind, in the words of St. Paul; it cannot be secured by our effort but can only be received in love. This desire is the reward of fidelity and a gift that God promises to every humble believer. No matter what our intellectual capacity or educational background, another tier of wisdom is always waiting for us. God stretches our desire to seek that wisdom, to seek himself, through the gift of intellect.

MEANS OF INTELLECTUAL FORMATION

PERSONAL MEANS

196 The most important means of growing in the intellectual dimension is very practical: establishing regular habits of personal study. St. Francis de Sales called study the "eighth sacrament" in the life of the priest.[163] There is simply no substitute for doggedly setting aside time for daily reading, making it a priority, and using it effectively. In the busy life of a priest, this is no easy task. Our daily goal cannot be so trivial that we make no progress, but neither can it be so ambitious that we soon grow discouraged. Even fifteen or twenty minutes a day is often enough to keep alive the spark of intellectual growth.

---

162 "Let no one think that it is enough for him to read if he lacks devotion, or to engage in speculation without spiritual Joy, or to be active if he has no piety, or to have knowledge without charity, or intelligence without humility, or study without God's grace, or to expect to know himself if he is lacking the infused wisdom of God." St. Bonaventure, quoted in PDV, no. 53.

163 St. Francis de Sales, quoted in E. J. Lajeunie, *Saint Francis de Sales: The Man, the Thinker, His Influence,* vol. 2 (Bangalore, India: S. F. S. Publications, 1987), 36.

197   As priests, our primary intellectual interests will likely be in the areas of theology, catechesis, and apologetics. Twenty centuries after Christ, we can be sure that we will never run out of worthwhile material. The DMLP mentions several categories: "The first place among reading materials must be occupied by Sacred Scripture; followed by the writings of the Fathers, the Doctors of the Church, the ancient and modern Masters of spirituality, and by the documents of the *Magisterium of the Church*, which constitute the most authoritative and updated source of ongoing formation; the writings and the biographies of saints will also be most useful."[164]

198   A privileged place in our topics for study should be given to the Holy Scriptures, which the Second Vatican Council calls the "soul of sacred theology."[165] By attentive study of the Bible,[166] as well as the great commentaries and sermons of the Fathers and other faithful interpreters, we can come to a better understanding of the sacred texts and more fruitfully share them in our preaching and teaching. As the Council reminds us: "In the sacred books, the Father who is in heaven meets His children with great love and speaks with them; and the force and power in the word of God is so great that it remains the support and energy of the Church, the strength of faith for her sons, the food of the soul, the pure and perennial source of spiritual life."[167]

199   The primary theme of study for the priest will therefore be drawn from the content of the faith. Nevertheless, a priest also does well to include in his study regimen, at least periodically, material with a

---

164   DMLP, no. 105 (emphasis original).

165   Second Vatican Council, *Dei Verbum (Constitution on Divine Revelation)*, no. 24, in *The Documents of Vatican II*, ed. Walter M. Abbott (New York: Corpus Books, 1966). Subsequently cited as DV.

166   "I would like to speak first to the Church's ordained ministers, in order to remind them of the Synod's statement that 'the word of God is indispensable in forming the heart of a good shepherd and minister of the word.' Bishops, priests, and deacons can hardly think that they are living out their vocation and mission apart from a decisive and renewed commitment to sanctification, one of whose pillars is contact with God's word." Benedict XVI, *Verbum Domini*, no. 78.

167   DV, no. 21.

cultural, historical, artistic, or scientific focus. These sources might derive from a priest's own intellectual interests or aim at broadening his knowledge of certain social themes. They can keep him grounded in the important trends of the age, assist him in his work with souls, and provide illustrations and matter for his preaching.[168]

200 It may be very helpful regularly to provide an output for one's study, such as guiding an adult formation program or a Bible study. Teaching the faith can result in the priest-teacher growing in his own faith.

FRATERNAL MEANS

201 As is the case with any human virtue, the habit of study is strongly influenced by the example and encouragement of those around us. Priest friends who take seriously the intellectual life will help us sustain good academic habits with their encouragement, affirmation, and accountability. This support happens informally through ordinary conversations when friends share the fruits of their reading with each other. The exchange of interesting intellectual ideas with friends is one of the great joys in life, a way to expand our own horizons, and— even more significantly—a means to spur the friendship toward new depths of mutual understanding and affection.

202 More formally, fraternal groups can also contribute to our ongoing intellectual formation. Many priests take part in theological or book discussion groups on a regular basis. By jointly selecting the material to discuss, such groups give direction to priests who might otherwise be unsure of what to read. By holding each other accountable, they

---

168 "In order to be a good guide of his People, the priest is also to be attentive to the signs of the times; from those that have to do with the universal Church and its journey in the history of man, to those closest to the concrete situation of a particular community. This discernment calls for constant and correct updating in the study of the sacred sciences with reference to diverse theological and pastoral problems, and the exercise of a wise reflection on the social, cultural and scientific data characteristic of our present day and age." DMLP, no. 78.

give motivation to priests who are striving to build a regular habit of study. Above all, such groups enrich participants by promoting a lively discussion of important ideas, further reinforcing the benefits of a flourishing intellectual life.

EPISCOPAL MEANS

203 There are many ways that a diocesan bishop can foster the ongoing intellectual formation of priests. He can, first of all, give personal testimony to the importance of ongoing study, publicly sharing the fruits of his own reading. Priest gatherings, convocations, and study days are ideal opportunities for him to speak about the habit of study. He might wish to touch on what he has been studying; work it into talks, homilies, and pastoral writings; or simply discuss it with priests during parish visits.

204 A diocesan bishop can also host study days for priests that, at least occasionally, address deeper theological topics.[169] Such meetings can be more formal, perhaps including an address by a prominent theologian or author and allowing time for questions and discussion. They can also be simple and relaxed affairs, for example by inviting any interested clergy to discuss a thought-provoking article from a theological journal around a meal or before a social gathering.

205 Another way for a diocesan bishop to nourish the intellectual life of his priests is by providing material for their own ongoing formation. The diocese can encourage personal study, for instance, by offering an annual reimbursement for academic expenses, such as the purchase of theological texts and subscriptions to academic journals. The diocese can also partner with outside institutions to adapt study materials to

---

169 "It would be necessary above all to deepen understanding of the principal aspects of priestly existence by referring in particular to biblical, patristic, theological and hagiographic teachings in which the priest must be constantly updated not only by reading good books, but also by attending study cours-es, conferences, etc." DMLP, no. 94.

the life of the priest, offering free registration for those interested. Finally, by sending priests for advanced studies in theology or other disciplines when he discerns such study is warranted, the diocesan bishop fosters the intellectual formation of the entire presbyterate by demonstrating his commitment to theological and intellectual life as well as by adding a local resource who can share his expertise with brother priests and the broader Church (e.g., a seminary), as recommended by the Second Vatican Council.[170]

---

170 The "bishops must be concerned that some persons dedicate themselves to a more profound knowl-
     edge of theological matters. Thus there will never be any lack of suitable teachers to train clerics,
     and the rest of the clergy as well as the faithful can be assisted in providing themselves with needed
     teaching. Thus, too, will be fostered that wholesome advancement in the sacred disciplines which is
     altogether necessary for the Church." PO, no. 19. See also CIC, c. 819.

CHAPTER SIX
Pastoral Formation

206 Each area of ongoing priestly formation is important, but the pastoral dimension enjoys a certain primacy. After all, Jesus identifies himself as the Good Shepherd—the Good Pastor—and this image, more than any other, should inform the life of his priest:[171]

> I am the good shepherd. A good shepherd lays down his life for the sheep. A hired man, who is not a shepherd and whose sheep are not his own, sees a wolf coming and leaves the sheep and runs away, and the wolf catches and scatters them. This is because he works for pay and has no concern for the sheep. I am the good shepherd, and I know mine and mine know me, just as the Father knows me and I know the Father; and I will lay down my life for the sheep. (Jn 10:11-15)

207 Contrasting Jesus with a hireling is instructive. Unlike the hired hand, Jesus lays down his life for his sheep. Unlike the laborer, Jesus protects his sheep against the wolves. Unlike the worker, his motive is not material gain but rather charity, concern for the sheep. He cares for them and wants the best for them. Finally, unlike the hired hand, Jesus knows his sheep and they know him.

208 These lessons can easily be applied to the priest. We are called to model our life after that of the Good Shepherd. When St. John Vianney identified the priesthood as "the love of the Heart of Jesus," he was not simply being poetical. In a real sense, the priest must incarnate the love of the Good Shepherd in the midst of the People of God.

---

171 "Through the sacramental ordination conferred by the imposition of hands and the consecratory prayer of the Bishop, there is established in the presbyterate 'a specific ontological bond which unites the priest to Christ, High Priest and Good Shepherd' (PDV, no. 11)." DMLP, no. 2.

We too must lay down our life for our sheep, protect them against wolves, care for them with loving concern, and know them and be known by them.[172] In the words of the Second Vatican Council, as priests assume "the role of the Good Shepherd, they will find in the very exercise of pastoral love the bond of priestly perfection which will unify their lives and activities."[173]

209 The first three dimensions of formation—human, spiritual, and intellectual—converge in the pastoral dimension.[174] The human nature of the priest needs to be well formed so that it constitutes "a bridge and not an obstacle for others in their meeting with Jesus Christ."[175] The spiritual life of the priest ensures that his ministry is rooted in a deep interior union with Jesus the Good Shepherd. The intellectual life of the priest forms his mind to grasp the saving truths of the faith and to hand them on faithfully, nourishing his people with "pure spiritual milk" that will help them "grow into salvation" (1 Pt 2:2). All these dimensions of formation, culminating in the pastoral, orient a priest toward the salvation of souls and pastoral charity. In whatever part of the vineyard a priest is asked to exercise his ministry, he will find that applying himself to ongoing pastoral formation will yield much fruit in his own life and in those entrusted to his care.

---

172 "Pastoral charity constitutes the internal and dynamic principle capable of uniting the priest's multiple and diverse pastoral activities and bringing men to the life of Grace. The ministerial activity must be a manifestation of the charity of Christ, whose bearing and conduct the priest will know how to project, and this unto the ultimate donation of self for the good of the flock entrusted to him." DMLP, no. 54.
173 PO, no. 14.
174 See PDV, no. 57.
175 PDV, no. 43.

MARKERS OF THE PASTORAL DIMENSION
Freedom for Ministry

210 The first marker of pastoral formation is the absence of glaring interior barriers to priestly ministry. These might be human barriers: for instance, compulsive behaviors, unhealthy relationships, narcissistic tendencies, or an escapist disposition to feed on entertainment and distraction. They can also be spiritual barriers, such as interior superficiality, scrupulosity, or a frenetic activism. A priest who does not find his joy in Christ, after all, frequently tries to find it instead in exterior accomplishments or comforts. These human and spiritual barriers all represent forms of slavery that prevent a priest from living in freedom and that limit his pastoral effectiveness.

211 Interior freedom is also a necessary condition for healthy celibacy, obedience, and simplicity of life. Celibacy, as we observed in chapter three, is primarily not a renunciation but a positive choice, a new and powerful way of loving more broadly. To be free, a priest must break with attachments that suffocate the charismatic grace of celibacy.[176]

212 Obedience is not a slavish conformity to the will of a superior; it is a humble and mature embrace of legitimate authority. It includes practical obedience to the diocesan bishop and loyalty to the Holy Father and the teachings of the Church.[177] It cannot flourish in a

---

176 "Consecrated to Christ in a new and excellent way (see PO, no. 16), the priest must therefore be well aware that he has received a gift from God, which, sanctioned in its turn by a precise juridical bond, gives rise to the moral obligation of observance. Freely assumed, this bond is theological and moral in nature before being juridical, and is the sign of that spousal reality coming to be in sacramental Ordination." DMLP, no. 58.
"Through his celibate life, the priest will be able to fulfill better his ministry on behalf of the People of God. In particular, as he witnesses to the evangelical value of virginity, he will be able to aid Christian spouses to live fully the 'great sacrament' of the love of Christ the bridegroom for his spouse the Church, just as his own faithfulness to celibacy will help them to be faithful to each other as husband and wife." PDV, no. 50.

177 "Since the priestly ministry is the ministry of the Church herself, it can be discharged only by hierarchical communion with the whole body. Therefore, pastoral love demands that acting in this communion, priests dedicate their own wills through obedience to the service of God and their brothers. This love requires that they accept and carry out in a spirit of faith whatever is commanded

heart that is turned inward in pride and insecurity. In addition, obedience involves an openness to serve the Church in whatever capacity the diocesan bishop asks and a willingness, as he is able, to learn other languages or develop new pastoral skills. Last, simplicity of life can take root only in a heart freed from the grasping demands of materialism, consumerism, and other disordered affections.[178] Uprooting these vices, so common in the modern world, is a precondition for a fuller embrace of simplicity of life and preparation for priestly ministry.[179]

213 The first marker of pastoral maturity, then, is the freedom to live as a man for others; to be chaste, humble, and simple; and to live as a shepherd prepared to defend his sheep from the wolves and care for them with an authentic and Christlike love.

SPIRITUAL SONSHIP

214 A second marker of pastoral formation in a priest is the eager embrace of our primary vocation to Christian discipleship. To be good spiritual fathers, priests must first be good spiritual sons.

---

or recommended by the Sovereign Pontiff, their own bishop, or other superiors." PO, no. 15. See also CIC, c. 273.

178 "Each priest is called to live the virtue of poverty which consists essentially in consigning his heart to Christ as the true treasure, and not to material things. The priest, whose inheritance is the Lord (see Nm 18:20), knows that his mission, like that of the Church, takes place in the midst of the world and that created goods are necessary for the personal development of man. Nonetheless, he will use such goods with a sense of responsibility, upright intention and detachment proper to him who has his treasure in heaven and knows that everything is to be used for the edification of the Kingdom of God (Lk 10:7; Mt 10:9-10; 1 Cor 9:14; Gal 6:6) (see PO, no. 17; John Paul II, General Audience, July 21, 1993, no. 3)." DMLP, no. 83.

179 "Lastly, even though the priest does not make a public promise of poverty, it is incumbent upon him to lead a simple life and abstain from whatever may smack of worldliness, thereby embracing voluntary poverty in order to follow Christ more closely. In all aspects (living quarters, means of transportation, vacations, etc.) the priest is to eliminate any kind of affectation and luxury. In this sense the priest must battle every day in order not to lapse into consumerism and the easy life that pervade society in many parts of the world. A serious examination of conscience will help him to assess his tenor of life, his readiness to attend to the faithful and perform his duties; to ask himself if the means and things he uses respond to true need or if he may not be seeking convenience and comfort, taking flight from sacrifice. Precisely at stake in the consistency between what he says and what he does, especially with respect to poverty, are the priest's credibility and apostolic effectiveness." DMLP, no. 83. See also CIC, c. 282 §1.

When priests fail to remember that they are beloved sons of God,[180] disciples of Christ before all else, they easily lapse into the errors of clericalism. Moreover, since they share in the priesthood of the very Son of God himself, it is fundamentally important that they be deeply aware of being "sons in the Son" and share in his outlook and desires. Priests will then be ready, with all the force and attractiveness of their personality and personal witness, to communicate the love of Christ to those whom they serve, as spiritual fathers and good shepherds.

Primacy Given to Salvation of Souls

215 One of the defining features of a man called to the priesthood, a necessary quality of his interior and apostolic life, is a desire for the salvation of souls. St. John Vianney, the patron saint of parish priests, expressed his own burning desire when he boldly prayed to God, "Grant me the conversion of my parish; I consent to suffer whatever you wish, for as long as I live."[181] The heart of a priest is therefore marked by a generosity in his service to others, zeal in the apostolate,[182] and qualities of pastoral charity such as patience, compassion, mercy, and a desire to reconcile sinners to God.[183] He endeavors to follow the guidance provided in the First Letter of St. Peter, which encourages priests about the need to serve in humility and self-forgetfulness: "I exhort the presbyters among you, as a fellow presbyter and witness to the sufferings of Christ and one who has a share in the glory to be revealed. Tend the flock of God in your midst, [overseeing] not by constraint but willingly, as God would

---

180   See DMLP, no. 3.
181   St. John Vianney, quoted in St. John Paul II, "The Cure of Ars" (Letter to All the Priests of the Church for Holy Thursday 1986), CatholicCulture.org, July 11, 2023.
182   "In the image of the Apostles, apostolic zeal is the fruit of the overwhelming experience issuing forth from closeness with Jesus." DMLP, no. 21.
183   "He will also know how to bend over with mercy upon the difficult and uncertain journey of the conversion of sinners, to whom he will reserve the gift of truth and the patient, encouraging benevolence of the Good Shepherd, who does not reprove the lost sheep, but loads it onto his shoulders and celebrates its return to the fold (see Lk 15:4-7)." DMLP, no. 41.

have it, not for shameful profit but eagerly. Do not lord it over those assigned to you, but be examples to the flock. And when the chief Shepherd is revealed, you will receive the unfading crown of glory" (5:1-4).

216   Such a priest desires to understand the interior dispositions of those he serves and to accompany them on their road to holiness. "A priest who is close to his people," Pope Francis said in his 2018 Chrism Mass homily, "walks among them with the closeness and tenderness of a good shepherd; in shepherding them, he goes at times before them, at times remains in their midst and at other times walks behind them. Not only do people greatly appreciate such a priest; even more, they feel that there is something special about him: something they only feel in the presence of Jesus."[184] He is not satisfied with being a mere caretaker or maintainer of an institution but strives with holy ambition to plant the faith more deeply in the hearts of his people and to evangelize those who do not yet know Christ. In fact, his gaze extends beyond the confines of his immediate apostolate to the needs of the whole Church, because "every priestly ministry shares in the universality of the mission entrusted by Christ to His apostles."[185]

217   Because the primary means of fulfilling the priest's evangelical mission is through the sacraments, an important marker for pastoral formation is a love for administering them faithfully, reverently, and generously, especially the Mass and the Sacrament of Penance.[186] A priest can find no more effective way to promote the salvation of souls.[187] Beyond the sacraments, he faithfully intercedes for the people

---

184   Francis, Homily, 2018 Chrism Mass, March 29, 2018.

185   PO, no. 10.

186   "The ministry itself, by which the priest brings Christ's redemptive gifts to his people, transforms the priest's own life. In a particular way, the celebrations of the sacraments lead the priest to a holy encounter with God's all-transforming, merciful love." PPF, no. 41.

187   "While the service of the Word is the fundamental element of the priestly ministry, its heart and vital center is undoubtedly the Eucharist, which is above all the real presence in time of the one and

he serves.[188] He brings them and their needs before the Lord every day, confident that his priestly vocation is meant for their spiritual regeneration and has a special claim on God's blessing. He has a particular desire to foster vocations to the priesthood, diaconate, and consecrated life, seeing in such work a privileged and grace-filled opportunity to multiply his efforts to spread the Gospel.[189]

218 As priests, we should know our parishioners. Our engagement with our congregation informs our preaching and forms us. There is a reciprocal relationship in a priest's preaching: I give to feed the congregation, and what I receive from the congregation feeds me. This bond is fluid and continual: "The homily is the touchstone for judging a pastor's closeness and ability to communicate to his people. We know that the faithful attach great importance to it, and that both they and their ordained ministers suffer because of homilies: the laity from having to listen to them and the clergy from having to preach them! It is sad that this is the case. The homily can actually be an intense and happy experience of the Spirit, a consoling encounter with God's word, a constant source of renewal and growth.[190]

219 In his preaching, the priest confidently hands on the life-giving Gospel in all its integrity, the "primary duty" of a priest according to

---

eternal sacrifice of Christ. Sacramental memorial of the death and resurrection of Christ, real and efficacious representation of the singular redeeming Sacrifice, source and apex of the Christian life and all evangelization (see PO, no. 5; SC, nos. 78, 84-88), the Eucharist is the beginning, means and end of the priestly ministry, since 'all ecclesiastical ministries and works of the apostolate are bound up with the Holy Eucharist and are directed towards it' (ibid.). Consecrated in order to perpetuate the Holy Sacrifice, the priest thus manifests his identity in the most evident manner." DMLP, no. 66.

188 "They themselves will take special care in celebrating the Eucharist with the full awareness that, in Christ and with Christ, they are the intercessors before God, not only to apply the Sacrifice of the Cross for the salvation of humanity, but also to present to divine benevolence the particular intention entrusted to them." DMLP, no. 69.

189 "It is 'a necessary requirement of pastoral charity' (PDV, no. 74), of love for one's priesthood for each priest—ever docile to the grace of the Holy Spirit—to be concerned about inspiring vocations to the priesthood that may continue his ministry at the service of the Lord and for the good of humanity." DMLP, no. 43. See CIC, c. 233.

190 Francis, *Evangelii Gaudium (On the Proclamation of the Gospel in Today's World)*, November 24, 2013, no. 135. See also USCCB Committee on Clergy, Consecrated Life, and Vocations, *Preaching the Mystery of Faith: The Sunday Homily* (Washington, DC: USCCB, 2012).

the Second Vatican Council.[191] He strives to make his preaching clear, convincing, and attractive, conscious that he is communicating the beautiful truth of God's loving plan for humanity.[192] He also ensures that the content of his preaching and teaching adheres faithfully to the doctrine of the Church and that his mind is formed *sentire cum ecclesia*, "to think with the Church."[193] In communicating God's saving truth, the priest is sympathetic to his people's perspective and their cultural sensibilities so he can speak to them in a way they can readily embrace.[194] Especially in an age that seems ever more distant from the peace of Christ, faithfully preaching the whole Gospel will come at a cost. He will inevitably meet with resistance. However, for a priest who wishes to be a courageous shepherd, it is essential that he be willing to appropriately expose himself to risks to protect the flock. Here, too, the image of Jesus the Good Shepherd is the model. When Jesus calls himself the "gate" to the sheepfold (Jn 10:7-9), he is referring to the ancient practice in which a shepherd sleeps in the gap of the stone wall that protects the sheep. The shepherd literally guards the sheep with his own body in the dark of the night. It is an apt image of the priest to this day. As St. John Vianney observed, "If a pastor remains silent when he sees God insulted and souls going astray, woe to him! If he does not want to be damned, and if there

---

191 PO, no. 4.

192 "In this [contemporary] context the priest must above all revive his faith, his hope, and his sincere love for the Lord, in such a way as to be able to present Him to the contemplation of the faithful and all men as He truly is: a Person alive and fascinating, who loves us more than anyone else because He gave His life for us: 'A man can have no greater love than to lay down his life for his friends' (Jn 15:13)." DMLP, no. 46.

193 See St. Ignatius of Loyola, *The Spiritual Exercises of St. Ignatius Loyola, Spanish and English, with a Continuous Commentary*, trans. Joseph Rickaby (New York, NY: Benziger Brothers, 1923).

194 Helpfully instructive documents on the vital importance of the liturgical context of preaching are the Congregation of Divine Worship and the Discipline of the Sacraments's 2015 *Homiletic Directory* and the USCCB's 2012 document *Preaching the Mystery of Faith: The Sunday Homily*. Both documents insist upon the vital importance not only of preaching on the scriptural readings but of "virtually always" linking these to the celebration of the Eucharist that follows. In a very practical way, priests' assimilation of both documents would improve priests' preaching and continually allow them to be formed by the liturgy. Furthermore, meditation on liturgical texts such as the second reading in the Office of Readings can lead to a powerful union of personal prayer and preaching. As St. Thomas Aquinas observed, "That form of active life in which a man, by preaching and teaching delivers to others the fruits of his contemplation is more perfect than the life that stops at contemplation." *Summa Theologicae*, III, q. 40, art. 1 ad 2.

is some disorder in his parish, he must trample upon human respect and the fear of being despised or hated."[195]

A Heart Open to All

220 A final marker of pastoral formation in the life of a priest is a magnanimous openness to other souls. He must be a man for others.[196] Such a disposition reveals itself in a priest's life in many ways. Of primary importance is a pastoral zeal that is open and free of constraints. In forming his Apostles for their priestly ministry, Jesus begins and ends with a fishing expedition (see Mt 4:18-22 and Jn 21:1-14). He invites them, and each of us: "Come after me, and I will make you fishers of men" (Mt 4:19). The faithful priest is therefore dedicated to the work of evangelization; he extends himself to reach those who do not know Jesus or who have fallen away from his Church. An evangelically committed priest will not be content to simply receive whoever comes to the parish but will actively promote efforts, in his own life and among his parishioners, that have proven effective in drawing souls to the Lord.[197]

221 Such a priest will also be generous in his service to those who are poor, elderly, lonely, abandoned, or rejected and to others on the peripheries of society.[198] His deep concern for social justice is motivated not only by temporal needs but above all by supernatural

---

195   St. John Vianney, quoted in St. John Paul II, "The Cure of Ars" (Letter to All the Priests of the Church for Holy Thursday 1986).

196   "If the priest lends to Christ, the Most Eternal High Priest, his intelligence, his will, his voice and his hands so through his ministry he may offer to the Father the sacramental sacrifice of redemption, he is to embrace the dispositions of the Master and, like him, live as a *gift* for his brothers. He is therefore to learn to unite himself intimately to the offering, placing on the altar of the sacrifice his whole life as a revealing sign of God's gratuitous and prevenient love." DMLP, no. 66, emphasis original. So too, it is good to remember that the priest was first ordained a deacon and, as such, was conformed to Christ the Servant. The priest must never forget this diaconal aspect of his ministry.

197   See, for example, CIC, c. 528 §1, pertaining to the parish pastor.

198   "Friend of the poorest, he will reserve his most refined and delicate pastoral charity for them, with a preferential option for all the old and new poverties so tragically present in the world, ever recalling that the first misery from which man must be liberated is sin, the ultimate root of all evil." DMLP, no. 83. See CIC, c. 529 §1.

ends: the salvation of souls.[199] A wideness of heart and a broadness of mind enable him to work readily and competently with people from different cultures, outlooks, and theological and ecclesial points of view.[200] This work includes openness to the unique, popular cultural Catholic traditions among diverse Catholic populations. He is particularly keen to address deep-seated injustices such as racism and other chronic prejudices. He can work in different ministerial settings, for instance among youth and young adults as well as the elderly; he is comfortable in multicultural environments. He is collaborative in his ministry, respectfully and gratefully working shoulder to shoulder with lay people, deacons, and religious men and women. Finally, he is actively engaged in the wider community, outside the confines of his parish and the members of his congregation, seizing opportunities to work with ecumenical, interreligious, and civic associations.

222 The Church offers many examples of holy priests who exemplify the gift of self to their flock. Blessed Michael Joseph McGivney, during his thirteen years of ministry, spent his priesthood in parish ministry and established the Knights of Columbus to build unity and charity. And Venerable Augustus Tolton heroically overcame many obstacles to offer his life as a priest to the Church. He was born an enslaved person but was brought into freedom by his mother a year after the Civil War ended. He was denied entrance into seminary in the United States, so he was sent to Rome, where he completed his studies, thinking he would become a missionary to Africa. Upon ordination, he returned to the United States and ministered to both African Americans and European Americans in his parish— something unheard of at the time in a segregated world. He went

---

199 See CIC, cc. 222 §2 and 287 §1.

200 "A distinctive manifestation of this dimension in building up the Christian community consists in transcending any particularist attitude: in fact, priests must never place themselves at the service of a particular ideology insofar as this would wane the efficacy of their ministry. The priest's relationship with the faithful must always be essentially priestly." DMLP, no. 41.

from being someone's property to becoming a shepherd whom other pastors questioned because his preaching was attracting people from not only other parishes but both races. Fr. Tolton is a model for priests of every era, but especially for those who feel persecuted or isolated.

223 Both of these parish priests suffered personal struggles, from slavery to a virus outbreak, from losing the family breadwinner to studying abroad. Both were called by God to serve diverse populations; they both "knew the smell of their sheep" and recognized the signs of the times. The priest today is invited to find in Fr. McGivney and Fr. Tolton inspiration and challenge. They offer inspiration to live life with greater pastoral charity. Following their heroic example and challenge can help us let go of anything that does not conform to serving the Lord and his people. These priests give us great examples of what can be accomplished when we give without counting the cost.

MEANS OF PASTORAL FORMATION

PERSONAL MEANS

224 The strongest pastoral foundation for priestly work is a life of discipleship and holiness. It is important for priests, as disciples ordained for ministry, to enter fully into the lives of people and understand the challenges they face. In the Parable of the Good Samaritan (Lk 10:25-37), Jesus reminds us that the love of neighbor means getting close to the other and making the other's problems one's own. Pope Francis echoes this: "It is important to maintain contact with the people, with God's faithful people, because there is the anointing of God's people: they are the sheep. By losing the smell of the sheep, by distancing yourself from them, you can be a theorist, a good theologian, a good philosopher, a very good curial official who does all the things," but you will have lost "the ability to smell

the sheep."[201] Forming relationships with the poor, migrants and refugees, and others through the St. Vincent de Paul Society, Catholic Charities, Catholic Relief Services—in other words, forming human relationships with those on the margins and those with whom he might be uncomfortable—helps a priest in his ongoing growth in all dimensions.

225 Many of the means of ongoing formation already mentioned in the human and spiritual dimension also strengthen a priest's pastoral work. After all, though a priest spends much of his day doing the work of God, he must still conform his heart to the good work that he is doing.[202] He therefore strives to embody the markers of the pastoral dimension in an intentional, generous way. He sanctifies his priestly work by consciously uniting it to the Lord, rectifying his intention as often as needed so that he gives greater glory to the Father.[203] He is above all attentive to his life of prayer and other spiritual practices that foster his union with God, through whom his pastoral activity is made effective.[204] He may work to develop the habit of a daily examen to discern God's hand at work in his ministry and express gratitude for that grace.

---

201 Francis, quoted in "Pope Francis: 'Priests Must Be Close to the People,'" *Vatican News*, October 26, 2022.

202 "Are you in charge of a parish? If so, do not neglect the parish of your own soul, do not give yourself to others so completely that you have nothing left for yourself. You have to be mindful of your people without becoming forgetful of yourself." St. Charles Borromeo, *Acta Ecclesiae Mediolanensis* 1599, 1178, quoted in Office of Readings for the Memorial of St. Charles Borromeo (November 4), *Liturgy of the Hours* (1974).

203 "The assimilation of the pastoral charity of Christ in order to make it become a form of his own life is a goal that requires the priest to live an intense Eucharistic life, as well as continuous efforts and sacrifices, since this charity cannot be improvised, knows no breaks, and cannot be considered as attained once for all. The minister of Christ will feel it his obligation to live and bear witness to this reality always and everywhere." DMLP, no. 54.

204 "Born of these prayers and called to renew in a sacramental and bloodless manner a Sacrifice inseparable from them, priests will keep their ministry alive with a spiritual life, to which they will give absolute pre-eminence, avoiding any neglect due to other activities." DMLP, no. 49.

226 Saintly priests through the ages testify as well to the power of a priest's ascetical practices in his pastoral work.[205] Every day the priest approaches the altar of God and kisses the place of Christ's sacrifice. Doing this reminds him that he is called to live out that sacrifice in his own life as both priest and victim, in union with the High Priest. "Loving the Cross in a hedonistic society is a scandal," the DMLP observes, "but from a perspective of faith it is the fount of interior life. The priest must preach the redemptive value of the cross with his style of life."[206] As the bishop exhorts the ordinands in the Rite of Ordination, "Understand what you will do, imitate what you will celebrate, and conform your life to the mystery of the Lord's Cross."[207]

227 For personal sacrifices to enrich his pastoral work, a priest needs to make some practical resolutions. At times, and with the approval of his spiritual director, he may wish to employ more demanding ascetical practices, as St. Paul wrote to the Corinthians: "I do not fight as if I were shadowboxing. No, I drive my body and train it, for fear that, after having preached to others, I myself should be disqualified" (1 Cor 9:26-27).[208] Such sacrifices, in addition to their potential benefit to the priest himself, may be the best way to advance his pastoral work. To a priest who complained that his apostolic zeal was bearing no fruit, St. John Vianney suggested, "You have offered humble prayers to God, you have wept, you have groaned, you have sighed. Have you added fasts, vigils, sleeping on the floor, castigation

---

205   As leaders of the community, priests "ideally cultivate the asceticism proper to a pastor of souls, renouncing their own conveniences, seeking what is profitable for the many and not for themselves, so that the many may be saved. They are always going to greater lengths to fulfill their pastoral duties more adequately. Where there is need, they are ready to undertake new pastoral approaches under the lead of the loving Spirit who breathes where He will." PO, no. 13.
206   DMLP, no. 67.
207   Roman Pontifical, *Ordination of a Bishop, of Priests, and of Deacons*, no. 135.
208   The Greek word for "drive" here refers to severe, even harsh, discipline, such as that used by a boxer preparing for a match.

of your body? Until you have done all of these, do not think that you have tried everything."[209]

228　In addition to these extraordinary measures, a priest offers sacrifices for his people in ordinary ways every day. Self-denial, after all, is an essential component of discipleship. "Whoever wishes to come after me," Jesus insisted, "must deny himself, take up his cross, and follow me" (Mt 16:24). In the life of a priest, such mortifications also reinforce his pastoral ministry. Small self-denials at meals, patient submission to illnesses and other sufferings, kindness and patience with tiresome people, the cheerful omission of small comforts, and other little crosses—those that he voluntarily chooses and those that he encounters in the course of a day—can all be occasions to encounter the Lord, offer him our love, and intercede for God's people. Perhaps the most important self-denial a priest can practice is simply keeping his hand on the plow and doing his work faithfully and without fanfare, day after day.[210] These ingredients of fidelity and perseverance in the priesthood make up the recipe of genuine joy in pastoral ministry.

229　A final personal means of growth in the pastoral dimension is analogous to ongoing formation in other professions: namely, training in ministerial skills.[211] A priest can take advantage of many opportunities for professional development and tailor his studies to his own needs. By broadening his knowledge of various ministries, for example, he can stretch his pastoral abilities and widen his experience. By developing better leadership skills, he can improve his governance of the parish. By learning new management skills in areas

---

209　St. John Vianney, quoted in St. John XXIII, *Sacerdotii Nostri Primordia*, no. 72.

210　"The priest should act under the impetus of a receptive and joyful spirit, the fruit of his union with God through prayer and sacrifice, which is an essential element of his evangelizing mission of becoming all for everyone (see 1 Cor 9:19-23) in order to win them over to Christ." DMLP, no. 46.

211　See PPF, nos. 268, 288.

such as finance, human resources, and organization, he can become a more able administrator and manager of the temporal goods of the Church. In addition, the priest can find a great deal of guidance and formation from the many people he is serving, including the parish staff, the various councils and commissions, the volunteers, and other organizations in the parish. The laity involved in these groups bring talent and expertise that a priest is wise to acknowledge and learn from. The priest may also wish to take advantage of the expertise of his bishop's collaborators in the curia.

Fraternal Means

230 Brother priests help each other grow in the pastoral dimension in many ways. Priest friends can encourage, affirm, and hold each other accountable for personal growth in holiness as well as pastoral generosity and competence.[212] Such friendships are most helpful when they stimulate intentional conversations about pastoral methods, the care of souls, preaching, and the handling of difficult pastoral situations. Even friendships that have less explicitly apostolic origins, such as those emerging from common human interests, can foster priestly conversation. Such friends find that they have lost none of their common interests while they put their friendship on an even deeper and more stable foundation: their mutual growth as Christians and as priests.

231 Mentoring relationships can also be a powerful means to grow in the pastoral dimension of formation. Fraternal consultations with seasoned priests give younger priests an opportunity to draw from the wisdom of experience and avoid many pitfalls to which they are otherwise prone. Priests willing to receive and give such assistance

---

212   It is particularly recommended that groups of priests read and discuss the DMLP.

contribute meaningfully to the overall health of a presbyterate and foster a fruitful unity among priests of different age groups.

232 Last, every diocese has a great deal of pastoral experience, and certain priests will be especially effective in particular ministries. When a priest is given a new assignment, he can find it helpful to make on-site visits to priests successfully doing similar work, learning from them on the ground.[213] In addition, those who serve in similar capacities— for instance, those involved in campus ministry, hospital work, or military or prison chaplaincy—might consider gathering periodically to share best practices and speak about particular situations they face. They can be means of ongoing formation for each other, as well as a source of encouragement and new friendships.

EPISCOPAL MEANS

233 Because ongoing pastoral formation often consists of gaining new knowledge or revisiting matters previously learned, diocesan bishops and dioceses can do much to foster this dimension of priestly life. Many subjects can be addressed in priest study days, workshops, convocations, and online seminars. Topics that lend themselves to such training may be grouped under three principal headings: priestly ministry, parish apostolates, and management.

Priestly Ministry

234 As in any other field, priests sometimes need to return to basics, refresh their memory, and update their knowledge about daily duties. Liturgical training, especially in regard to the celebration of Mass and other sacred rites, can often be helpful. So too can formation

---

213 "In view of his own spiritual and pastoral growth and out of love for his flock, the priest should welcome with gratitude, and even seek on a regular basis, the orientations of his bishop or the latter's representatives for the development of his pastoral ministry. It is also an admirable practice for the priest to request the opinions of more expert priests and qualified laypersons with respect to the most suitable pastoral methods." DMLP, no. 33.

on the Sacrament of Penance and Reconciliation, such as exploring ways to help penitents overcome habitual sins or reminding priests of the various reserved penalties, faculties for their remission, and their relationship to the sacrament. Methods to strengthen homiletics skills are always welcome, as is concrete assistance in giving spiritual direction, preparing couples for marriage, and performing other priestly duties.[214]

235 Some priests find that a temporary shift away from direct parish ministry can be highly restorative. Though such a break can be a sacrifice for dioceses already coping with a shortage of priests, giving some men an opportunity to enrich skills and pastoral experience can be a good way to provide long-term personal development and enable them to return to parish ministry more motivated than ever. Such opportunities could include, for instance, working for a time as a chaplain, taking an extended sabbatical, or enrolling in short courses on topics such as bioethics, liturgy, canon law, or deliverance ministry. Opportunities could also include more intense, direct work with the poor and marginalized or even a period doing missionary work at home or abroad.

236 The field of pastoral counseling offers many opportunities for ongoing formation. A workshop offering an overview of psychology from the perspective of Catholic anthropology could be very helpful. Knowing how to approach specific issues such as depression, suicide prevention, and troubled marriages can be critical in providing accompaniment and Christ-centered consultation. Of equal importance is recognizing when an issue is beyond the priest's scope

---

214 "Particularly interesting may be the organization of courses or seminars on the apostolate of the Sacrament of Confession or on practical questions of spiritual direction in both general and specific situations. Practical formation in the field of the liturgy is also particularly important. Special attention should be reserved to learning how to celebrate the Mass well—as pointed out earlier, the *ars celebrandi* is a *sine qua non* condition of the *actuosa participatio* of the faithful—and to adoration outside the Mass." DMLP, no. 96.

of expertise, so that referral to professional services is appropriate. In the complex field of medical ethics, seminars can bring priests up to date on bioethical questions such as end-of-life issues. Many such examples would be useful for the ongoing formation of priests.

Parish Apostolates

237 Effective pastors are always on the watch for ways to build up their parochial apostolates. Ongoing formation can play an important role in this search for best practices in parish leadership. At the broadest level, the parish must evangelize and equip parishioners for their own outreach.[215] An in-depth study of the lay vocation and its largely untapped potential for works of evangelization and mercy, for instance, could help pastors carry out their own work of formation. So too could a workshop on using social media and other digital resources more effectively, or a workshop on catechizing with apologetics resources that address challenges to the faith with clarity and compassion. Other topics for discussions on best practices include guidance for ministering to youth and young adult groups; preparing catechumens and candidates for reception into the Church; promoting priestly, diaconal, and consecrated vocations; reaching out to non-Catholics; and working with ecumenical groups. Any work of a typical parish, in fact, likely profits from canvassing effective priests and presenting the findings to the presbyterate as a whole.

Management

238 Functional and administrative topics of study can be helpful to pastors and those preparing to become pastors, whose managerial duties seem always to be expanding. One general topic for formation might be leadership skills, especially for priests responsible for

---

215   See CIC, cc. 528 §1 and 529 §2.

schools or parishes with large staffs. Management principles—such as those associated with "high reliability organizations"—can prepare priests for the inevitable crisis. Another broad but crucial topic is the effective collaboration of priests with the lay faithful in the administration of a parish. More specific topics for training can include ways to benefit from parish and finance councils, fiscal accountability and responsibility, the handling of sensitive personnel issues, and advice on how to maintain a physical plant. Last and perhaps most specific of all, workshops on personal organization and time management may be particularly helpful to young priests and new pastors who feel overwhelmed by the many demands on their time.

APPENDIX A
Program *for* Newly Ordained Priests

239 This appendix concerns the crafting of strategies and programs for the ongoing formation of recently ordained priests (those in their first five years after ordination).[216] It does not offer a ready-made program or even a template for a program. Presuming that dioceses are varied and have varied geography, resources, and personnel, we offer the ideas that follow to assist those who have the responsibility to discern and to plan.

PRELIMINARY OBSERVATIONS

240 We do not need to provide the data here to demonstrate the importance of the first three years after ordination for the long-term well-being of a new priest and for the effectiveness of his priestly ministry. Numerous studies have covered this ground and provide ample evidence for the need to pay particular attention to this period of a priest's life, as he moves from formation into the exercise of priestly ministry.

241 The transitional nature of this period provides one of the first challenges to those responsible for ongoing formation. Newly ordained priests may fear that ongoing formation programs may be mere continuations of seminary formation. As this document asserts, a clear relationship does indeed exist between formation before ordination and lifelong engagement in ongoing formation. A seamless transition from one to the other, with a steady commitment to ongoing growth and development as a man and as a priest, is a

---

216 Studies indicate the importance of the first five years after ordination. However, many priests are already considered as candidates for a pastorate by their second or third year. In addition, most dioceses would have difficulty sustaining a program for five years. Therefore, this appendix suggests a program of one to five years to allow for flexibility given local circumstances.

reasonable goal. Nonetheless, the ongoing formation program for the newly ordained needs to acknowledge and honor the change that has occurred in them and in their lives with the gift of priestly ordination. This balance can be difficult to achieve. For example, a healthy program needs a degree of accountability for those who miss scheduled gatherings or arrive late. On the other hand, such enforcement starts to look like life in the seminary. The best outcome is a program that draws the men in by the quality of its content and fraternal engagement. The encouragement and support of the diocesan bishop, as spiritual father, is also helpful. Priests are more receptive to the wishes of their diocesan bishop when he communicates them clearly and convincingly.

242 With these observations in mind, and in light of the *Guide's* focus on the importance of fraternity in ongoing formation, fraternal time and engagement are essential components and tools of an ongoing formation program for the recently ordained. For similar reasons, those responsible for the program's content need to consult the men concerning the topics and the quality of presenters and be responsive when there is feedback. The same need may shape simple program decisions. For example, the priest director for the program or programs should not be the only one who preaches or presides. The men themselves should be asked to participate in programming by volunteering to celebrate the Mass, lead a Holy Hour, or lead one of the hours of the Liturgy of the Hours. The quality of the hospitality is also critical. The goal is to put new clergy at ease and give them opportunities to engage with one another.

PART 1: KEY LEADERSHIP IN THE ONGOING FORMATION OF THE RECENTLY ORDAINED PRIEST

243 As this *Guide* indicates, the most important figure in ongoing formation is the priest himself. His humble self-awareness of the need for continuous conversion and growth is the essential ingredient for the effectiveness of any program in his life.

THE DIOCESAN BISHOP

244 This document continually emphasizes the role of the diocesan bishop in ongoing formation. This importance is especially acute in the case of the recently ordained. These first years build upon and strengthen the relationship between the priest and his diocesan bishop that formed during the priest's years of initial formation. Ongoing formation programming helps the new priest understand his place in the wider mission of the diocese and helps him recognize the link between the exercise of his ministry and that of his diocesan bishop. The programming also helps the diocesan bishop get to know his new priests better and gain insights for their future work and assignments. Above all, he exercises a fatherly role to encourage, admonish, and guide his spiritual sons. Although it may not be reasonable for the diocesan bishop to take part in every aspect of the ongoing formation of the recently ordained, his absence would seriously diminish its mission. In large dioceses the diocesan bishop might call upon auxiliary bishops to assist; but in all cases, the plan should directly involve the diocesan bishop and give him time with the new priests.

THE PASTOR

245 The first assignment of the new priest has long-term effects upon his life and ministry. Care must be exercised in assigning new

priests—especially in determining the pastor(s) who will be their immediate guide(s) in their first years. In this, the pastor is a delegate of the diocesan bishop himself. The pastor must offer a model of a selfless, disciplined, authentic, and effective priest of Jesus Christ. He needs to examine the maturity of his own words and actions and be aware of the lessons he communicates. Some pastors who are effective in their leadership might not be good candidates for the role of pastor to a recently ordained. The diocesan bishop needs to avoid pastors with strong ideological biases or contempt for the younger clergy. The pastor need not be a buddy to the new priest, but he must have a sense of humility before the insights and interests of a new generation. He is charged not to mold the man in his own image but to help mold him in the image of Jesus Christ, the High Priest.

246 Training pastors for this role is also important. Even if they do not attend the ongoing formation programming, they form a critical element in the ongoing formation team. At the least, the pastor needs to understand and support the rationale of the program and help the new priest to plan his time well so that he will be able to take part in program events. Ideally, the program also offers pastors training for their role in supervising the young priest in his first years. Some pastors identify their role in this regard as being mentors, but this is a misunderstanding of the term (see below under "The Mentor"). The role of a mentor is primarily supportive. Although a pastor can and should be supportive, the heart of his contribution is supervisory. He helps the young priest to find the balance of ministry and prayer, work and rest. He helps the man understand accountability and his responsibility to others and to the mission. He offers concrete feedback on preaching and work performance. He also bears the burden of communicating serious concerns to the diocesan bishop, or to his delegate, if a young priest struggles with alcohol, substances,

improper engagement with media, or other behaviors that endanger him or others.

The Spiritual Director

247   The role of the spiritual director and confessor is critical in the life of every priest. As this matter is a personal choice of the individual priest, assigning a spiritual director is not necessary (as it might be in the seminary). Nonetheless, those charged with crafting and overseeing the program of ongoing formation need to ensure that newly ordained priests understand the importance of establishing this habit of regular direction from the very start of their priestly ministry. Although this unique relationship takes place in the internal forum, and the discussions are entirely confidential, the fact that a priest has a director and is faithful to direction is not in the internal forum; it is a legitimate interest of the diocesan bishop or his delegate. A diocese or several dioceses in concert may find it advisable to arrange the training of suitable directors to assist young priests in establishing the practice from the start.

The Mentor

248   The mentor is a seasoned or mature priest, other than the pastor, who provides peer support from one priest to another. The mentor for a recently ordained priest should be a mature priest who lives and works in a parish other than that of the new priest. As opposed to the priest's own selection of a spiritual director, the diocesan bishop may wish to assign mentors to newly ordained priests (some programs do permit the new priest to nominate individuals to serve as mentor). The rationale for assigning mentors is to avoid the possibility that a new priest might select a friend and cloud the nature of the mentorship role. In addition, the mentor works with the new priest

under the authority of the diocesan bishop, who has the right to judge the suitability of the mentor. Ideally, the diocese could provide a workshop to train mentors. Such training could be combined with the training of mentors for new pastors or international priests. The diocesan bishop will also find it advisable to consider the selection process for the mentor during the assignment process for a new priest. The mentor should not live or work at such a distance from the new priest's assignment that meeting regularly would be burdensome. In addition, the assignment process will involve discussion of the new priest's talents and qualities—a conversation that assists in the matching of an appropriate mentor. It is vital that the mentor relationship be established at the outset of the new priest's ministry. The role of mentor does not take place in the internal forum, but it does have a high expectation of confidentiality. Exceptions to that expectation would involve grave matters such as those involving risk or danger to the new priest or to the people he serves.

The Director

249 Dioceses have varying levels of resources and practices with regard to ongoing formation. Some may have part-time or full-time dedicated directors of ongoing formation. In other settings, the vicar for clergy or the priest personnel director may oversee ongoing programs for the recently ordained. For this general outline, we simply observe that the kind of program envisioned here requires careful planning, oversight, and engagement. Ideally, the program would have a dedicated director. In appointing leadership for the ongoing formation of new priests, diocesan bishops need to consider the capacity of the potential leader to foster and practice fraternal regard among the new priests and for the new priests.

PART 2: KEY PROGRAMMING IN THE FORMATION OF THE RECENTLY ORDAINED PRIEST

250 As noted in the preliminary observations to this appendix, fraternal interaction is an essential element to the effectiveness of engagement with recently ordained priests. Any and all programming proposed below should include opportunities for fraternity and communal prayer. Educational programming should make use of insights from adult education. With adults, mere lecture is far less effective than programming that incorporates discussion and case studies. The program also needs to allow participant feedback and be responsive to that feedback. Content that draws upon experience is especially effective with adult learners.

RETREATS AND TIMES OF RECOLLECTION

251 Many young priests look forward to the opportunity to participate in a diocesan retreat or to plan their own retreat after ordination. A retreat with the other new priests in the first years is a valuable tool for building fraternity and helping young priests to form the habit of an annual retreat. The choice of director or preacher for a group retreat is very important; planners will wish to consult young clergy about which preachers move them. In this instance, and in crafting the content of other areas of the program, planners need to understand and respect the perspectives of the new priests. Although presbyterates sometimes experience "generation gap" tensions in matters such as liturgical style or clerical attire, the retreat is not the place to attempt to "fix" the new priests or indoctrinate them into the perspective of their elders. The content of the retreat is a good place to address some challenges of the first years of ministry from biblical and spiritual perspectives. In addition to the retreat, for these same reasons, the diocese is advised to plan one or two days of recollection for recently ordained priests in the first years.

ATTENTION TO PHYSICAL HEALTH AND EMOTIONAL WELL-BEING

252 Studies indicate that Catholic priests in the United States of America contract chronic illnesses in middle age at twice the rate of the general population. In part, this high rate is due to factors like high stress, low physical activity, and ignorance of proper nutrition. Programming for the recently ordained should assist new priests in establishing good nutritional habits as well as incorporating physical activity into their schedules. These programs might link individuals to already existing resources in the diocese, such as a Catholic clinic or volunteer medical professionals. Planners may also incorporate programs for the group such as healthy cooking classes. Including health club membership fees as a benefit for priests may encourage newly ordained priests to develop exercise habits early in their priesthood.

253 The next section specifically addresses topics related to the emotional well-being of the new priest. Generally, however, all of those charged with responsibility for ongoing formation need to be attentive to signs of emotional distress in a new priest. The pastor and mentor have a particular responsibility to be vigilant for signs of isolation, angry outbursts, severe procrastination, substance abuse, or any other indications that a new priest may be struggling emotionally. Part of the work of pastors and mentors is to help a new priest be self-reflective in this regard and committed to the well-being of his peers.

PASTORAL AND HUMAN FORMATION

254 Planners need to consider what topics should be addressed in the first years of a new priest's ministry and then create tools to address these topics. In this planning, again, they will find it vital to draw from adult learning models. Adults learn best in participatory models. The most effective manner of instruction for adults is concrete practice.

Therefore, in finding presenters, planners should seek practitioners and experts who will give the men the opportunity to bring their concrete experiences for questions and discussion. Other tools such as case studies, group problem solving, and discussion are also effective with adults. These techniques—along with being reluctant to simplify issues and prompting priests to evaluate programs, even when things are going well—promote the establishment of dynamic and strong practices and minimize the possibility of problems. Any given diocese has educators who can offer advice in crafting these methods for the program.

255 Although the following is not comprehensive, here are some key conversation topics for the ongoing pastoral and human formation of new priests. The relative weight and order of the topics need to be considered in light of the seminary programs attended by the men.

    a. Marriage, marriage preparation, and the pre-judicial or pastoral inquiry prior to a petition for a declaration of invalidity of marriage[217]

    b. Canon law case studies for pastoral life

    c. Intercultural competency

    d. Homiletics and preaching

    e. Time management and life balance

    f. Whole-hearted commitment to one's assignment without accepting additional responsibilities which detract from it

    g. Discernment regarding readiness for additional responsibilities, such as offering spiritual direction, leading retreats, and so on[218]

    h. Personal grief and pastoral care of the grieving

---

217 See Francis, *Mitis Iudex Dominus Iesus (By Which the Canons of the Code of Canon Law Pertaining to Cases Regarding the Nullity of Marriage Are Reformed)*, August 15, 2015, arts. 2-3.
218 See PPF, nos. 43, 229r, 340, 381-382.

i. Relationships with permanent deacons and lay ecclesial ministers

j. Cultivation of good relationships and boundaries with staff

k. Good confessional practices

l. Relationship between the priest and his diocesan bishop; relationships within the presbyterate

m. Moral theology "hot topics" and strategies for dealing with controversy

n. Proper use of media and engagement in social media for ministry

o. Chastity and celibacy as practically lived in priestly life

p. Effective engagement with children and teens in light of the Church's sexual abuse crisis

q. Pastoral boundaries within the establishment of social friendships with parishioners

Special Consideration

256 Those charged with supervising programs for the recently ordained may wish to incorporate insights from the Congregation for the Clergy's 2013 *Directory for Ministry and the Life of Priests* into the programming content. Ideally, the new priests should read this document at least once during the program. Presenters should be well aware of the document.

Orientation for Pastors and Mentors

257 As explained above, the pastor and mentor are key relationships in the first years of a new priest's ministry. The diocese needs to offer orientation to those who exercise these roles so that their work is effective, consistent, and integrated into the entire program of ongoing formation. In both cases, part of the orientation will lay out the program and its expectations. Pastors need to prioritize the new priest's participation in the program, even if that means the new priest might be absent from parish ministry to attend the programs.

Mentors likewise need to have a sense of the whole program and a willingness to commit to meeting with their mentees approximately monthly (a minimum of ten meetings per year is recommended). As noted in part one of this appendix, the role of the pastor is supervisory, and his orientation needs to make the case for this approach. In the case of the mentor, the role is a matter of peer support. Mentors need guidance in avoiding the temptation to become an advocate for the mentee or an intermediary in ministerial disputes.

258 The pastor and the mentor are key monitors of engagement in the larger program. Their work will be assisted if the program provides rubrics for growth in ministry.[219] Both pastor and mentor need to attend to any signs of physical, emotional, or spiritual distress in the new priest. On the positive side, this attention means encouraging regular spiritual direction and prayer, exercise, and healthy living. When the pastor or mentor notes danger signs such as isolation, depression, anger, or substance abuse, he needs to bring those concerns to the man and to the delegate of the diocesan bishop. In preparing mentors and pastors for their respective roles in peer support and supervision, planners may find it useful to consider already existing programs or collaboration with other dioceses.

FINAL NOTE

259 The elements described in this appendix require considerable effort, resources, and commitment on the part of a diocese. Where geography permits, dioceses may find it advisable to join in shared efforts. For those crafting the ongoing formation program, seminary formation programs and several national and regional ongoing formation programs offer useful resources and advice.

---

219 Rubrics offer characteristics or qualities that serve as goals and wayposts in ongoing formation. In categories such as homiletics, ministry with youth, pastoral care of the sick, and so on, the rubrics offer concrete descriptions of a skilled practitioner in these areas. The sixth edition of the USCCB's *Program of Priestly Formation* is a useful resource in developing these rubrics.

APPENDIX B

A TOOL *to* EVALUATE WHEN *a* PRIEST REQUIRES ASSISTANCE

260 At the end of initial formation, diocesan bishops and their delegates generally know their priests and can provide them with appropriate support and guidance. However, over time everyone experiences the accumulative effect of various pressures that affect physical, psychological, and spiritual health. The key is to recognize and cope with stressors, so that their impact may be negligible.

A PRIEST'S HEALTH INVENTORY

261 This inventory invites a priest to comment as needed within five areas: physical health, emotional health, social support, ministerial environment, and spiritual health.

PHYSICAL HEALTH PROBLEMS

262 **Eating:** Eating too much or too little is not uncommon with a mood problem, such as anxiety, depression, or general difficulty with modulating emotions. Two key issues to evaluate are (a) the percentage of weight lost or gained unintentionally and (b) the loss of control over eating decisions. A 5 to 10 percent change in weight can indicate depression or significant anxiety.

263 **Sleeping:** Although the need for sleep varies greatly, a priest who consistently gets an hour or two more or less than is normal (for that person) or who struggles with falling asleep or staying asleep might have a mood disorder. In addition, people who regularly self-medicate to sleep often need referral.

264 **Exercise:** Everyone should exercise. However, many priests choose not to. The key concern centers on a priest's decision to decrease his exercise significantly. He should be asked why. If he expresses a lack of energy and loss of pleasure in life, this development might indicate depression. If he feels less fit to exercise, a medical referral may be indicated.

265 **Substance Use:** Smoking and alcohol consumption are not uncommon for priests. Questions a diocesan bishop might raise include the following: Has there been an increase in substance use? How much and for how long? Anyone who regularly consumes multiple alcoholic drinks a day should be asked to discuss his drinking patterns. Any use of illegal drugs or abuse of prescription drugs is a red flag. If even one person has suggested that a member of the clergy has a problem with substance use, the matter should be investigated.

EMOTIONAL HEALTH PROBLEMS

266 **Mood Issues:** Any ongoing, intense experiences of depression, anxiety, impulsiveness, obsessions, or compulsions indicate the need for a referral.

267 **Anger Issues:** If a priest has discouraging or upsetting experiences, how does he handle them? Aggressive behaviors need to be weighed according to the following factors: Can he speak objectively about his behavior after the fact? Is he able to focus primarily on his own shortcomings? Are the level and frequency of aggression of concern to others?

268 Empathy Issues: Being able to share feelings when appropriate and not to share when not appropriate—according to the nature of a relationship—is a sign of maturity. If a priest is consistently unable to empathize with others, this inability is cause for concern. Also, if the priest consistently shares deep personal feelings with minors or others over whom he has an authority relationship, the situation should be investigated.

Social Support Problems

269 Supportive Relationships: All priests should be able to identify people who know them well and whom they trust. If they do not communicate regularly with their support persons, personally and by phone or video conferencing, this lack is cause for concern. Also, a priest who cannot identify someone with whom he can freely share in depth is at greater risk for succumbing to emotional problems.

270 Peer Relationships: All priests need supportive relationships with other clergy. Although some priests are comfortable being loners or prefer mixing with laity, they should at least be comfortable mixing with peers at official gatherings. A lack of peer relationships is cause for concern.

271 Pastoral Relationships: Effective shepherding of the flock requires establishing close relationships with parishioners. Although most often these develop into healthy friendships, sometimes they can evolve into unhealthy and emotionally charged relationships. Such a development can signal the abuse of power, temptations against chastity, and codependency. Such situations are not healthy for either individual.

MINISTERIAL ENVIRONMENT PROBLEMS

272 **Attitude Toward Ministry:** Burnout among priests occurs primarily when they lose interest in ministry. An interest level of 5 or below on a scale of 1 to 10 is of concern.

273 **Parish Staff Issues:** Staff shortages or frequent turnover can be cause for concern, as well as problems collaborating with parishioners, staff, fellow priests, diocesan personnel, and others.

274 **Relationships with Superiors:** It is important for a diocesan bishop or his delegate to consider whether a priest seems comfortable with him or anyone else in the leadership circle. A priest who is unable to communicate with the diocesan bishop or his delegates may simply be resistant; but if other concerns arise, the lack of a relationship can exacerbate the problem.

SPIRITUAL HEALTH PROBLEMS

275 **Prayer:** Priests who do not pray daily are at risk. Questions about actual time spent with Liturgy of the Hours, sacraments, and private prayer will help uncover the reality of how much prayer is a part of a priest's life.

276 **Sacramental Practice:** Priests who do not celebrate Mass daily unless assigned are depriving themselves of graces and of an intimacy with God that is particular to their vocation. Also, the failure to regularly make use of the Sacrament of Penance and Reconciliation makes a priest vulnerable to falls and could alienate him from God's mercy.

277 **Relationship with God:** A priest who articulates a true loss of faith or extreme distance from God needs a referral for a spiritual assessment.

278 Spiritual Direction: Many priests lack a spiritual director, a lack that is deleterious for one's vocational and ministerial health. However, if spiritual direction is regularly provided and significant problems persist, a spiritual assessment is indicated.

A PRIEST'S HEALTH ANALYSIS

279 The foregoing inventory provides an opportunity to analyze various sources of stress that can contribute to deterioration in physical, psychological, and spiritual health. After the priest writes out responses to each subtopic, reviewing them with an objective, balanced perspective is important. Rarely is the news all bad. After reflecting on both strengths and weaknesses, the diocesan bishop or his delegate needs to weigh this basic question: Is the priest managing the stress, or is stress managing him?

280 If stress has the upper hand and there are signs of dysfunction, then it is important to address those areas that need more attention. Sometimes the priest needs to simply change certain routines and set a few simple goals. However, the diocesan bishop or his delegate may find it necessary to request a referral for further physical, psychological, or spiritual assessment.

APPENDIX C

CULTURAL CONSIDERATIONS *in* ONGOING FORMATION

CONTEXT

281 It is a foundational truth that we all belong to the one family of the baptized. There is a need for conversion that would make ordained ministers see the immigrant and the international citizen for who they are: our brothers and sisters. Cultures may be diverse, as might histories and origins; but our Lord died to give each of us a new identity that all Catholics share.

282 Catholic priests serving in US dioceses are a culturally diverse body serving a diverse flock. This is not a new phenomenon. Some areas of the United States such as Florida, Texas, and California were already being evangelized by Spanish clergy for more than a hundred years before the establishment of the United States. In the British-controlled colonies on the Eastern Seaboard, early Catholic presence was limited by anti-Catholic restrictions. By the time the new US Constitution guaranteed religious liberty, some Catholic clergy were already active in the former colonies—notably in Maryland, Pennsylvania, and New York. Although some of the clergy were themselves born and raised on the Eastern Seaboard, more were missionary priests hailing from European countries.

283 The strong presence of missionary priests only increased in the nineteenth century, as the Catholic population itself began to change with the arrival of new immigrants. For a brief period in the mid-twentieth century, US dioceses saw a rise in vocations that tipped the balance in favor of local clergy. Even so, many of those local vocations were in fact produced among immigrant communities,

as the sons of immigrants responded to the call. More recently, the numbers have shifted again, as the rise in local vocations has subsided and US dioceses have begun to turn again to missionary priests to fill their ranks or to provide ministry to immigrant communities. US immigration patterns have also shifted in the twentieth century away from largely European immigration toward Latin American, African, and Asian immigration. The cultural diversity of missionary priests has therefore grown ever broader to include priests from all over the world.

THE POWER OF CULTURE

284 The cultural diversity of the Catholic Church in the United States, with its accompanying diversity of Catholic clergy, is a rich blessing to the life of the Church. Immigrant Catholics frequently bring renewal and new life to Catholic parishes, and the missionary clergy form a critical element of the pastoral care of US parishes and institutions. In addition, nonimmigrant members of the presbyterate reflect the varied background of the United States and add to the rich cultural expressions of the faith.

285 At the same time, we must acknowledge that this diversity also brings new challenges. Culture is a powerful force in human behavior and in the life of the Christian community. The nature of that power must be clarified, as the word "culture" is used to refer to several realities. In common use, it might evoke the particularities of dress, food, and custom among varied ethnic identities; or it might refer to the world of "high culture" such as museums, orchestras, and so on. This discussion does not focus specifically on these outward expressions of cultural identity. The concern here is with the basic underlying worldview and views that shape the perceptions and behavior of individuals. Social scientists frequently use the image

of the iceberg to visualize the visible outward expressions of culture that float above the surface, as well as the much larger body of culture hidden beneath the surface, where attitudes, perceptions, and behaviors find their origin. These aspects of culture may frequently be unexamined, even unconscious, motivators for behavior and judgments concerning others.

286 At issue is the worldview of the individual, shaped by a life immersed in a given culture. From that environment, an individual absorbs attitudes concerning the relative roles of old and young, male and female, clergy and laity. Here too is the foundation for the individual's outlook on critical matters like authority, conflict, rights and responsibilities, and so on. When unexamined, such attitudes frequently lead one to consider one's own viewpoint the norm, or the right way to think and act. For example, a priest from one culture might have a strong sense of deference to authority and therefore wait upon direction from his diocesan bishop or his delegate, while the diocesan bishop or delegate might misunderstand this cultural approach as being lazy or passive because his own culture places greater value on personal initiative. Cultural misunderstandings may be reduced or reconciled when individuals and communities examine their presumptions and dialogue with one another.

THE POWER OF FAITH

287 The Catholic Church, with its long history of experience with many cultures, has significant advantages in bridging divides. Of course, that experience is also set in a context of a faith that grappled early on with questions of cultural difference and came to the firm conclusion that God's plan calls human beings into communion, as one body, while leaving intact their uniqueness and diversity. If the pouring out of the Spirit at Pentecost may be seen as the healing of Babel, then note that the Babel experience made all alike, whereas Pentecost

united even as it respected the uniqueness of people's own languages and identities as Parthians, Medes, Elamites, and so on. The Catholic faith and its convictions provide the motivation to bridge cultural divides and the foundation for respect, even reverence, for differences.

CULTURAL ORIENTATION

288 When clergy arrive from other cultures as immigrant or missionary priests, they have a critical need for proper welcome and orientation to life in a new country and culture. This kind of programming, as essential as it may be, does not fall under the heading of "ongoing formation." The USCCB has already addressed this question at length in the 2014 edition of *Guidelines for Receiving Pastoral Ministers in the United States*.[220] Nonetheless, missionary priests serving in the United States do need to be considered by those planning for ongoing formation. First, missionary priests need opportunities specific to their needs as international priests. Even the most extensive orientation programming needs follow-up and amplification over time. New questions arise in the lived experience of international priests, and further discussion of culture is essential before a priest might be considered for a pastorate. Additionally, general programming needs to be accessible to priests of other cultures and should contribute to building up fraternal understanding and cooperation among priests from different cultural perspectives.

CULTURE AND ONGOING FORMATION

289 Three areas of concern center on the power and role of culture in ongoing formation efforts. First, all clergy have a general need for resources for intercultural competency in ministry to the diverse

---

220 USCCB Committees on Clergy, Consecrated Life, and Vocations; Cultural Diversity in the Church; the Protection of Children and Young People; Canonical Affairs and Church Governance, *Guidelines for Receiving Pastoral Ministers in the United States*, 3rd ed. (Washington, DC: USCCB, 2014). The document includes canon law, civil law, psychological considerations, and child and youth protection and safety considerations related to assessing and accepting pastoral ministers, as well as recommendations related to their reception, orientation, and ongoing formation.

Catholic population of the United States. Those same skills also have application to the interactions among clergy in rectories and in parish ministry. Second, dioceses need to consider the cultural identity of their presbyterate when selecting topics or planning programs for the clergy. This consideration benefits not only missionary clergy who were ordained in other countries, but also local clergy who might belong to a particular cultural identity within the US context. Third, the essential fraternity of a healthy presbyterate might be weakened if the clergy interact exclusively with those of their own cultural experience and viewpoint. A comprehensive ongoing formation program will seek to encourage or build those bridges between priests.

BOUNDARY EDUCATION

290 Given the nature of culture, attitudes and perceptions as to proper physical and emotional boundaries are heavily influenced by a priest's culture. Thus, boundary education (addressed in appendix D) needs to be sensitive to cultural differences among priests. For international clergy arriving for ministry in the United States, these concerns are a source of considerable anxiety. In addition to the initial orientation provided to them, this area of ongoing formation should figure into a number of settings for priests on a regular basis.

INTERCULTURAL COMPETENCY

291 The polarized and highly secular US context may make this aspect of ongoing formation more difficult, as the field of intercultural competency is sometimes characterized by ideologically driven jargon and operates from an anthropology that is foreign to Catholic culture. Some of the secular work has the regrettable effect of dividing people. Some clergy may be suspicious of these efforts because of such abuses, so this aspect of ongoing formation needs to be founded

upon the Church's biblically and theologically based anthropology. In that setting, the context is reverence for, and interest in, the other. This aspect of formation has an element of conversion, as individuals are asked to examine their presumptions and listen carefully to the experience of the other. The goal is to deepen understanding and empathy and to allow the insights that flow from that understanding to influence and modify behavior. Mindful of the above distinctions, a diocese may wish to draw upon some of the numerous resources and programs for intercultural competency in the United States.

292   Intercultural competency is a skill set essential to the ministry of all priests ministering in the US context, whether they are ordained for the local diocese or arrive from other countries. The US population (even more so the US Catholic population) is itself diverse. It includes immigrants from many countries, descendants of immigrants with ongoing subcultures, and distinct cultural identities that predate the establishment of the United States, such as Native populations, African American communities, and Hispanic/Latino communities.

293   Intercultural competency is also essential to the unity and fraternity of a presbyterate. Given this *Guide's* clear emphasis on the critical role of fraternity in the ongoing formation of priests, efforts need to be cognizant of, and responsive to, the gifts and challenges of culture. Understandably, people are often drawn to others with similar language and cultural viewpoints. On the other hand, healthy fraternity requires efforts to bridge those differences and provide settings where priests of different cultures learn and engage together.

LANGUAGE ACQUISITION AND
ACCENT MODIFICATION

294   The most dramatic form of intercultural competency comes when an individual learns a language other than his first language. Of course, the language ability is itself a key cultural skill. But learning a language has broader and deeper effects than meeting the practical need to communicate. To learn another language is to "get inside the head" of another culture and to experience different patterns of thinking. When, after much hard work, an individual progresses beyond the basic level of fluency, he develops new sympathy and even a bond with persons of the culture who speak that language. Opportunities for language study may address the needs of missionary priests outside the United States or US-born priests who need to learn a language or languages for ministry to US immigrant communities.

295   Accent modification is a related aspect of language ability. When a priest ministers in a language other than his own—for example, when a priest from a non-US but English-speaking country speaks with the accent of his homeland, or when a US-born priest learns an immigrant language—the man may need to modify his accent to promote the efficacy of his ministry. Two important observations concern accent modification. First, complaints that a given priest cannot be understood may be a subtle form of cultural rejection. In the US setting, people find it more acceptable to raise "accent difficulty" as an issue rather than express discomfort with the differentness of a priest from another culture. Curiously, when parishioners get to know a given priest, the complaints concerning accent diminish, even when the accent remains static. Therefore, when a diocese addresses concerns about accent modification with a priest, it needs to take care to reassure the priest that the issue concerns the efficacy of his ministry. Whatever his accent, his missionary contribution matters. Engaging early and effectively

with the people is just as important to his ministry as a program for accent modification. Second, accent modification is best addressed by speech pathologists and not by language instructors. Although language instructors might ask students to listen to and repeat words in the target language, speech pathologists possess the expertise and tools to assess the individual's formation of sounds and then teach exercises to modify how the individual makes the basic sounds that serve as the foundation for pronunciation in the target language.[221]

CULTURAL SENSITIVITY OBSERVATIONS

296 **Food and Hospitality:** The diversity of the US presbyterate has intensified. Whereas nineteenth-century US clergy might have come from a variety of European cultures, twenty-first–century priests come from every part of the world. In rectories, food can be a source of cultural conflict; missionary priests might find US cuisine unappetizing or unhealthy, and US-born clergy might object to the smells or flavors of foods from other places. The conflict points to the centrality of food tastes in culture. Most human beings have deep associations between food and home that form an important part of a sense of well-being. In addition, many cultures have strong ideas about the role of hospitality in acknowledging affection or the dignity of the other. If ongoing formation leaders wish to express their commitment to honoring the various cultures among a given presbyterate, then shaping the hospitality and menu to acknowledge and honor those cultures communicates a powerful sense of respect and belonging.

---

221 Speech pathologists who work with English speakers are widely available in the United States. US-based priests who study a language other than English may find it more difficult to identify a speech pathologist to assist them. In such cases, they may find it advisable to seek long-distance assistance using video technology. Accent modification assistance can be costly for a diocese and/or parish; the bishop will have to use his best judgment in helping his priests within his means.

297 **Language:** Although the diocese may not be able to offer programming in all the languages of a given presbyterate, if a significant number of the clergy come from one or more language groups, planners will find it useful to somehow acknowledge their presence. This might take the simple form of offering greetings in more than one language or including the language in the liturgy. In some instances, inclusion may mean developing an entire educational program or priest's retreat in a language other than English. Even those priests from other cultures who have worked in the US setting for years will appreciate the opportunity to pray and reflect in their first language, if it is not English.

298 **Program Topics:** Listening is a key component of intercultural competency. Any effective program will listen to its constituency in seeking presenters and selecting topics for programming. In a culturally diverse presbyterate, the listening must include priests from different cultures. The diocese is recommended to include priests from the various cultural groups of the presbyterate on any board or consultation for planning ongoing formation.

299 **Emotional Well-Being, Psychological Evaluation, and Therapy:** Psychological testing and therapy are culturally bound. If these tools are employed for priests who arrive in the United States from another country or who belong to a cultural subgroup within the United States, special care is necessary to avoid the pitfalls that may occur when a man is evaluated in a language other than his first language or is evaluated by a professional who lacks knowledge of his culture of origin. In such cases, it is possible to pathologize cultural attitudes. Evaluations might also be skewed, or therapy may not be as effective. Whenever possible, a priest should receive evaluation and care in his first language. When not possible, the evaluator or therapist at least needs familiarity with the man's culture of origin.

300 Special Note: While fraternity is a foundational factor for ongoing formation, and the diocese needs to build bridges across cultural divides, these points do not mean that a program should avoid culture or language-specific programming. Drawing together priests of a particular group for fraternity and formation can be an excellent tool promoting the overall goal of fraternity and effective ministry. Those who minister in another culture or find themselves a minority in a dominant culture need bonds with other priests who face similar challenges if they are to thrive in the wider environment.

CULTURE AND PLANNING

301 When planning intercultural competency programs or culturally aware general programming, the ongoing formation leadership needs to consider the cultural landscape of the local parishes and clergy. Of course, those in leadership need to understand the effects of their own cultural attitudes and have some sense of the worldview of the major cultures present in a given diocese. Among local communities and clergy, resources of expertise or lived experience may exist. For example, a long-serving international priest from Latin America might assist newly arriving priests in their first years of ministry. An effective pastor might be trained in the gifts and challenges of culture to serve as a mentor to a promising international priest. Small groups of the laity might serve as an ongoing support group for an international priest after he completes the orientation and training process. Small groups of clergy or individual international priests might serve in an advisory capacity to help the ongoing formation leadership plan content. All ongoing formation programming—even if the topic or program does not specifically relate to culture—needs to consider the power of culture in planning and shaping content.

APPENDIX D
BOUNDARY EDUCATION

302 The adoption of child and youth protection and boundary education programming in US dioceses, eparchies, institutes of consecrated life, and societies of apostolic life has been a remarkable achievement in the years since the 2002 establishment of the *Charter for the Protection of Children and Young People*. Safeguarding programs implemented for adults and youth have been foundational resources for a broad and rapid change in awareness of and vigilance in the protection of minors. For more than two decades, much has been learned about recognizing and preventing grooming behaviors and carefully supervising people, programs, and facilities. Experience with these tools has also deepened their effectiveness, even as the insights gained now offer possibilities for other kinds of boundary education. Although the protection of minors remains a priority, church leaders are increasingly aware that grooming behaviors and misconduct may be directed at adults and at vulnerable persons who might lack the capacity to protect themselves, even only occasionally.

303 In addition to the critical concern for the protection of the young and the vulnerable, then, the social sciences also propose that awareness of interpersonal boundaries is foundational to a healthy emotional life and to healthy relationships. Those boundaries may be physical, sexual, or emotional. This appendix addresses a variety of ways in which boundary education matters in the ongoing formation of priests.

HEALTH AND BOUNDARIES

304 As should be clear in the following paragraphs, the maintenance of healthy interpersonal boundaries begins with the priest's own balanced and healthy living. The priest who prays, engages in spiritual

direction, possesses appropriate and mature social skills, attends to good priestly fraternity and other healthy relationships, takes care of his health, and seeks to grow in holiness and affective maturity will have a good foundation for establishing and maintaining boundaries.

PROTECTION OF YOUTH

305 Dioceses, eparchies, and religious institutes provide foundational workshops and ongoing education in the protection of minors. By accessing a variety of source materials, priests can stay current in this quickly changing field. Priests' willingness to embrace safeguarding measures—especially in our schools and religious formation programs—sends a clear message to everyone that we value our youth and that maltreatment will not be tolerated. This safeguarding includes both the real and the virtual worlds.

PROTECTION OF VULNERABLE ADULTS

306 The safeguarding measures that protect youth also apply to vulnerable adults. It is important to know that church law changed in 2019 to clarify who belongs to this category of people. *Vos Estis Lux Mundi*, issued *motu proprio* by Pope Francis, defined a vulnerable person as "any person in a state of infirmity, physical or mental deficiency, or deprivation of personal liberty which, in fact, even occasionally, limits their ability to understand or to want or otherwise resist the offense."[222] With this the pope extended the definition beyond those with developmental or acquired disability. "Vulnerable adult" now includes an otherwise fully functioning person who may be under some form of duress and is thus deprived of personal liberty. Although youth protection programming may suffice for these concerns, it is essential to raise awareness of this comprehensive definition of vulnerable adults.

---

222   Francis, *Vos Estis Lux Mundi (You Are the Light of the World)*, May 7, 2019, arts. 1 §2b.

REPORTING

307 Priests are mandated reporters under canon law, subject to ecclesiastical sanction.[223] In addition, state and local governments establish legal requirements for mandated reporting of the abuse of minors (as well as vulnerable adults, in some cases). Given the variety of legislation even within a particular diocese or eparchy, those responsible for the ongoing formation of priests must determine the requirements and communicate them to the clergy. It should be noted that historically priests may have enjoyed a rather broad clerical exception to reporting laws. In many states the clerical exception has narrowed significantly in recent years. As these laws continue to change, those responsible for formation programs will need to monitor and communicate changes to the priests.

MINISTRY BOUNDARIES

308 To speak of boundaries when referring to ministry may seem strange. Ministry by its nature draws the priest into the lives and hearts of the people he serves. For this very reason, priests need ongoing formation opportunities to think and speak about the challenges inherent in sharing such important matters and moments in the lives of others. For example, a parishioner might misunderstand compassionate concern for something more personal. Any priest who has spent time in parish ministry has experienced a person in distress who lacks a sense of the boundaries in the relationship. In addition, there are risks for the minister as well if he himself is experiencing some kind of personal distress. His own need for affirmation or intimacy might cloud the ministerial relationship.

---

223 See Francis, *Vos Estis Lux Mundi*, art. 3 §1; CIC, c. 1371 §6.

WORKPLACE BOUNDARIES

309 There are similar pitfalls in the ministerial workplace. The typical parish staff is small, and the employees tend to spend a great deal of time together. Over time, they might fall into an easy familiarity. That same familiarity brings with it the risk of misunderstanding and even misconduct. Most regions of the United States have available training on boundaries in the workplace to help priests and staff avoid temptations such as favoritism or inappropriate behavior or conversation.

BOUNDARIES WITH ADULTS OUTSIDE MINISTRY AND THE WORKPLACE

310 Of course, it is possible for a priest to transgress boundaries with those outside ministry or the workplace. Ongoing formation programs need to include an honest assessment of the dangers of living chastely as celibate priests in a culture of easy and anonymous sexual contact—including behaviors that might be limited to digital settings.

BOUNDARIES IN THE PHYSICAL ENVIRONMENT

311 The demands of ministry in the current context of heightened concern for boundaries between adults, as well as ongoing concern for the protection of minors, require serious conversations about the physical layout of parish offices, confessionals, and clergy residences. This concern may be less a matter of boundary education and more a need for consultation with and awareness on the part of pastors. For example, many rectories lack a clear delineation between the priests' living quarters, the parish offices, and staff-accessible areas such as lounges or kitchens. For the sake of priests' privacy and a safe workplace, it is best to have clear boundaries within the rectory or office space. The confessional and any other place where priests meet

with individuals also need careful consideration.[224] Pastors need to give thought to clearly setting expectations about guests in rectories and about access to the private living quarters of individual priests.

PROFESSIONAL AND FINANCIAL BOUNDARIES

312 While the form varies from state to state, most US parishes have some kind of corporate structure in civil law. Canon law provides a similar juridical status as well as certain structures of consultation and approval for administrative and pastoral purposes. In the current environment of intensified scrutiny of the administration of parishes, dioceses, and eparchies, pastors must have proper formation in the expectations of civil law and canon law for consultation and accountability in administering the parish. Important considerations also relate to finance. Programming for ongoing formation needs to address the boundaries between the personal finances of the priest or pastor and the funds intended for the parish or related ministries.[225] When hiring or selecting contractors, pastors need ethical guidance concerning conflicts of interest for themselves and any other parish leaders. In the Internet age, when fundraising may be as simple as posting a crowdsourcing request, the clergy need ongoing formation in how money may or should be raised for worthy causes, including the accountability necessary to the process.[226] This education will be more effective if a diocese or eparchy considers developing written protocols for fundraising.

BOUNDARIES IN COMMUNICATIONS

313 This area is fairly broad, in that it includes concerns related to preaching, print publications (including the parish bulletin), interactions with traditional media, and engagement with social

---

224   See USCCB, "Complementary Norm to Canon 964 §2—The Confessional," October 20, 2000.
225   See, for example, CIC, cc. 531 and 1267.
226   See, for example, CIC, c. 1262, and USCCB, "Complementary Norm to Canon 1262—Fundraising Appeals," June 8, 2007.

media. In the culturally and politically polarized contemporary setting, priests need good ongoing formation in prudence, discretion, and the discipline of thinking and speaking on behalf of the Church. In the case of digital media, younger priests are more often familiar with using this technology. Some priests reared in the digital age might mix personal and pastoral use of digital media. In both cases the priest should be careful not to engage in aggressive or harassing communications. Digital and social media tend to absorb inordinate amounts of time and attention, serve as a distraction, and lower attention span. For this reason, priests need to be assisted to cultivate prudence in their use of media, so that their media usage serves the mission of the Church, and serves them, in healthy ways. The digital realm also poses significant risks to proper chaste living for the clergy. This too must be addressed in ongoing formation.